TEAM

Judy Garland: Beyond the Rainbow offers readers a vivid journey through the life of Judy Garland, one of the most enduring icons of the silver screen, presented with passion and insight by the ChatStick Team. This book goes beyond the glittering facade of Garland's public persona to explore the depth of her talent, the complexities of her personal life, and the legacy she left behind. Through a meticulous compilation of her life's story, the ChatStick Team weaves together the strands of Garland's career with her off-screen moments, revealing the woman behind the legend. From her early days in Grand Rapids, Minnesota, to her rise as a star in Hollywood's Golden Age, and her iconic role in The Wizard of Oz, this biography delves deep into the heart and soul of Judy Garland.

chatvariety.com

Our TEAM

In Judy Garland: Beyond the Rainbow, the ChatStick Team does not shy away from the challenges Garland faced, including her battles with addiction, her struggles with love and loss, and her quest for acceptance. Yet, it also celebrates her triumphs, her unparalleled talent, and her indomitable spirit that endeared her to millions worldwide. The book captures Garland's profound impact on the entertainment industry, her contribution to music, film, and her timeless influence on artists and fans alike. Through rich narrative and engaging storytelling, readers are invited to rediscover Judy Garland, the woman who fought bravely against the storms, and whose legacy shines as brightly as the rainbow she famously sang about.

chatvariety.com

table of contents

00
Introduction

01
Before the Rainbow

02
The Journey to Oz

03
Over the Rainbow

04
Beyond Oz: The Golden Years

05
A Star's Struggle

chatvariety.com

table of contents

06
The Later Years

07
The Icon Off-Screen

08
The Legacy Lives On

09
Reflections on a Legend

10
Conclusion: Beyond the Rainbow - Judy Garland's Everlasting Legacy

chatvariety.com

INTRODUCTION

chapter 01

Foreword by the ChatStick Team

In the world of literature, few names resonate as strongly as Judy Garland. Her talent, charisma, and enduring legacy have captivated audiences for decades. Judy Garland's journey, from her humble beginnings to her rise as one of the greatest entertainers in Hollywood history, is a testament to her unwavering dedication and the indelible impact she has left on the world.

Born Frances Ethel Gumm on June 10, 1922, in Grand Rapids, Minnesota, Garland grew up in a family deeply rooted in show business. Her parents, Frank and Ethel Gumm, owned and operated a theater called The New Grand Theatre, which showcased vaudeville acts and provided a creative outlet for the community. This theatrical environment nurtured Garland's curiosity and love for performing from a young age.

Recognizing their daughter's prodigious talent, Frank and Ethel Gumm began featuring the young Frances, who was affectionately called "Baby Gumm," in their shows. At the mere age of two-and-a-half, Frances made her stage debut, singing a heartfelt rendition of "Jingle Bells." From that moment on, it was clear that she possessed a rare gift that would shape her destiny. Her captivating performance garnered attention, and soon enough, Frances became a local sensation.

As the years passed, Garland's love for the stage and her passion for performing only grew stronger. She began taking formal vocal lessons, mastering her vocal range and technique under the guidance of local academy teachers. Alongside her vocal training, she devoted countless hours to dance lessons, honing her skills in ballet, tap, and jazz. Additionally, she studied acting and dramatic interpretation, immersing herself in the art of storytelling.

Despite her tender age, Garland developed a mature and powerful voice that belied her years. Her vocal talents blossomed and earned her widespread acclaim. She effortlessly transitioned across musical genres, ranging from lively show tunes to soulful ballads, and each performance resonated with an authenticity that touched people's hearts. Her ambition never waned, and she continued to seek out opportunities to improve her craft.

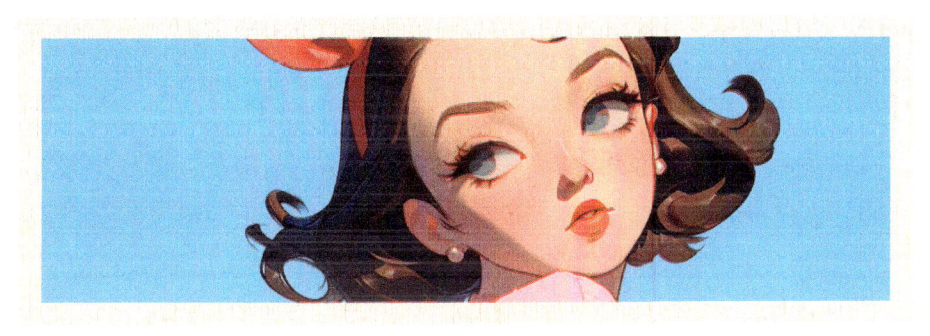

However, Garland's path to stardom was not without its challenges. Her family faced financial instability, at times struggling to make ends meet. The Gumm family's theater experienced occasional turbulence due to economic downturns and unforeseen circumstances. Yet, even in these difficult times, the family found solace in their shared love of performing. Despite financial uncertainty, Garland's determination never wavered. She embraced the stage as her refuge, pouring her heart and soul into every performance, knowing that her talent had the power to transcend her circumstances.

In 1934, tragedy struck the Gumm family when Frances' beloved father, Frank Gumm, unexpectedly passed away. This sudden loss sent shockwaves through the family and marked a turning point in young Frances' life. Determined to support her family and pursue her artistic dreams, Frances and her mother, Ethel, made the courageous decision to relocate to California in search of greater opportunities. It was during this transitional period that she officially changed her name to Judy Garland, taking her first name from a popular Hoagy Carmichael song and her last name from Broadway critic Robert Garland.

Garland's arrival in Hollywood marked the beginning of her ascent to stardom. She signed a contract with the renowned Metro-Goldwyn-Mayer (MGM) Studios, one of the most prestigious studios of the time, and began her journey towards becoming one of Hollywood's most iconic leading ladies. MGM recognized her extraordinary talent and beauty, swiftly casting her in a series of successful films as they meticulously crafted her image.

Garland's experiences at MGM shaped her into a consummate performer. She participated in intensive training programs, including vocal lessons, acting workshops, and dance rehearsals, under the studio's watchful eye. Her mentors and teachers nurtured her talent, guiding her through each aspect of her craft with precision and care. This rigorous education honed her skills, transforming her into a versatile and formidable force on the silver screen.

Throughout her career, Garland defied expectations and pushed boundaries, both on-screen and off. Her raw talent and vulnerability allowed her to inhabit a wide range of roles, captivating audiences with her versatile performances. From her emotive portrayal of Esther Smith in "Meet Me in St. Louis" (1944), where she immortalized the heartwarming song "Have Yourself a Merry Little Christmas," to her energetic and comedic turn in "The Harvey Girls" (1946), Garland showcased her unmatched artistic range. She effortlessly transitioned between drama, comedy, and music, establishing herself as a versatile actress and a natural-born entertainer.

Yet, Garland's success was not without its share of personal struggles. Her relationships were often turbulent and marred by failed marriages. In particular, her tumultuous partnership with producer and director Vincente Minnelli resulted in the birth of her beloved daughter, Liza Minnelli, who would later follow in her mother's footsteps as an acclaimed actress and singer.

Garland's enduring battle with substance abuse also plagued her personal and professional life. The pressures of fame, combined with a demanding work schedule imposed by the studio system, took a toll on her well-being. The expectations and scrutiny that came with being a Hollywood star pushed her to seek solace in the allure of drugs and alcohol. Despite these challenges, Garland's commitment to her craft remained unwavering. She continued to deliver breathtaking performances and captivate audiences, forever engraving her name in the annals of entertainment history.

As we embark on this journey through the life of Judy Garland, we invite you to explore the magic, the heartache, and the everlasting legacy of a remarkable woman. Through extensive research, personal anecdotes, and insights from those who knew her, we will uncover the trials and triumphs that colored Garland's life.

So, join us on this exploration of Judy Garland's remarkable life and career and discover why her name continues to shine as brightly as the stars she once graced on the silver screen.

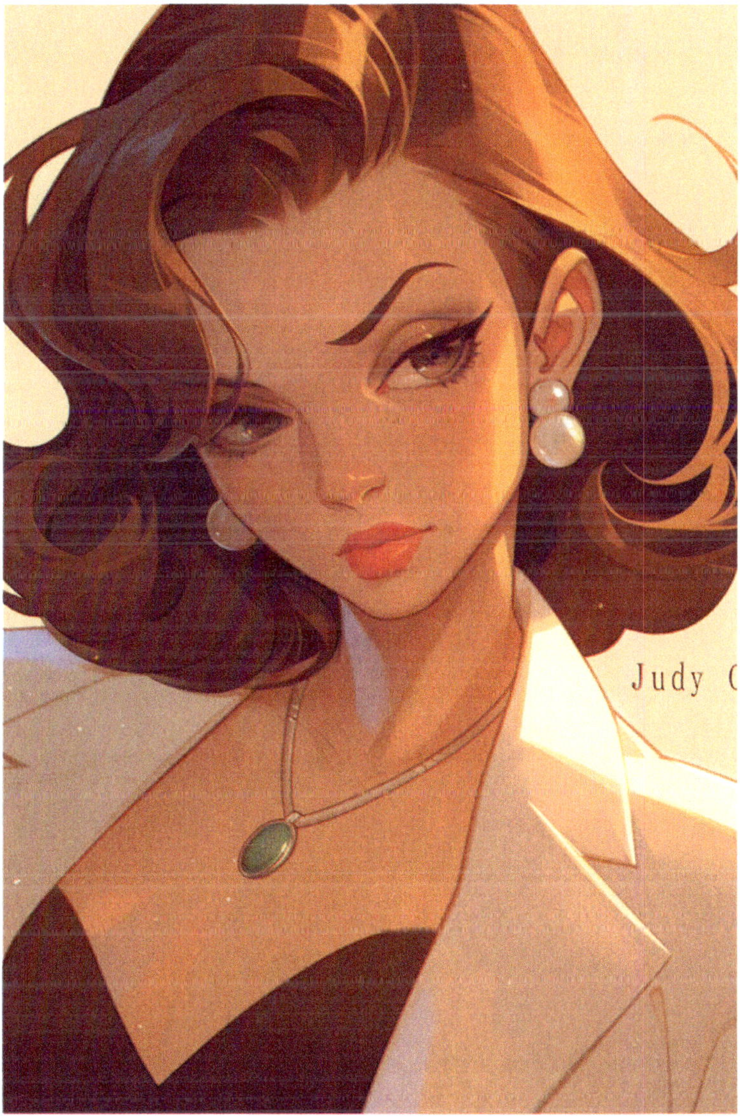
Judy

chapter 02

Judy Garland's place in Hollywood history

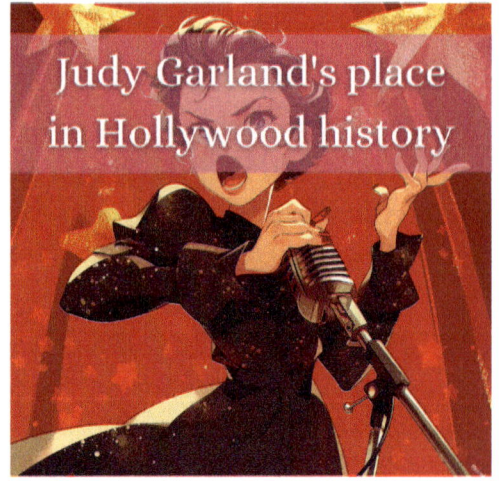

Judy Garland holds a significant place in the history of Hollywood. Her talent, charisma, and immense success not only made her one of the most celebrated actresses and singers of her time but also left a lasting impact on the entertainment industry.

From a young age, Garland showcased extraordinary talent, captivating audiences with her powerful voice and natural acting abilities. Born Frances Ethel Gumm on June 10, 1922, in Grand Rapids, Minnesota, Garland's journey to stardom began in the world of vaudeville. Alongside her sisters, she performed as part of the Gumm Sisters act, honing her skills and cultivating her passion for entertaining.

Garland's breakthrough role came in 1939 when she portrayed the iconic character Dorothy Gale in **The Wizard of Oz**. The role was a perfect showcase for her immense talent, as she sang one of the most memorable songs in film history, "Over the Rainbow." The song not only earned Garland an Academy Award nomination but also became her signature song, forever associated with her deep and emotive voice.

Throughout her career, Garland starred in numerous successful films, surpassing the boundaries of mere musicals. Her versatility as an actress was evident in movies such as **Meet Me in St. Louis** (1944), **The Harvey Girls** (1946), and **A Star Is Born** (1954). In the latter, she delivered a powerful performance that showcased the height of her dramatic range, earning her another Academy Award nomination.

But Garland's impact reached beyond the silver screen. Her live performances were transformative, transcending the boundaries of entertainment. Whether performing in concert halls or on television specials, Garland's captivating presence held audiences spellbound. From the moment she stepped onto the stage, all eyes were on her, and her raw, emotional performances resonated deeply with her viewers.

One concert that stands out is her legendary performance at Carnegie Hall in 1961. It was a defining moment in her career, showcasing not only her vocal prowess but also her ability to connect with the audience on a profound level. The concert was a phenomenon, with fans clamoring for tickets and a recording of the performance winning five Grammy Awards. It solidified Garland's status as one of the greatest live performers of her time.

However, Garland's life was not without challenges. Behind the scenes, she battled personal demons, including financial troubles, tumultuous relationships, and struggles with addiction. These demons took a toll on her mental and physical health, sometimes affecting her ability to perform. Yet, even in her darkest moments, Garland's talent shone through, delivering mesmerizing performances that touched the hearts of millions.

It is important to acknowledge the hardships she faced within the entertainment industry as well. Garland's early experiences with MGM were often challenging, as she dealt with intense pressure to conform to the studio's expectations of beauty and behavior. This led to personal insecurities and struggles with body image, which plagued her throughout her life. Despite these difficulties, Garland's resilience and determination allowed her to persevere and achieve remarkable success.

Garland's impact extended beyond her own career. She paved the way for future generations of performers, inspiring countless artists with her exceptional talent, determination, and ability to connect with audiences. Her influence on popular culture is evident in the numerous tributes and homages paid to her by contemporary artists, as well as the enduring popularity and cultural significance of her films and songs.

Tragically, Judy Garland's life was cut short on June 22, 1969, at the age of 47. Her passing was a great loss to the entertainment world, but her legacy lives on. Her performances continue to captivate and inspire audiences across the world. Judy Garland remains an enduring Hollywood icon, a symbol of talent, resilience, and the extraordinary power of raw emotion in entertainment.

In conclusion, Judy Garland's place in Hollywood history goes far beyond her immense talent and success. She left an indelible mark on the entertainment industry, captivating audiences with her powerful voice, exceptional acting skills, and genuine emotional connection. Despite the challenges she faced in her personal life and within the industry, Garland's contributions and influence continue to be celebrated, forever solidifying her status as a beloved icon in Hollywood's golden era.

Judy Garland

BEFORE THE RAINBOW

chapter 03

Early life and family background

Judy Garland, born Frances Ethel Gumm, on June 10, 1922, in Grand Rapids, Minnesota, came from a family deeply rooted in the entertainment industry. Her parents, Frank and Ethel Gumm, operated a theater where they showcased vaudeville acts, creating a vibrant and lively atmosphere that filled young Frances with wonder and inspiration. From the very beginning, she was surrounded by the magic of theater, engulfed by the allure of the stage and the power of performance.

As the youngest of three daughters, Garland often found herself in the shadow of her older sisters, Mary Jane and Dorothy, who were also talented performers. However, it was clear to those who witnessed her early efforts that Garland possessed a special spark, a combination of raw talent and unyielding determination that set her apart. Even at a young age, she had an innate ability to captivate audiences with her angelic voice and infectious charisma.

The Gumm family moved to California when Garland was still a child, in search of better opportunities in show business. They settled in Lancaster, a small town located in the Antelope Valley, where they continued to nurture their love for the entertainment industry. It was here that Garland's talent began to shine, as she performed alongside her sisters in their family troupe, known as "The Gumm Sisters." Their performances were met with enthusiasm and admiration, further fueling young Garland's desire to chase her dreams.

Despite her natural talent and love for performing, Garland's early years were not without challenges. Her parents' marriage faced strains, and she often found solace in her music and on stage. In those fleeting moments when she was lost in a song or dance, the troubles of the world melted away, and Garland felt a sense of purpose and belonging. She sang with a voice that resonated with a depth and emotion far beyond her years, a voice that would later become her signature.

Garland's dedication to her craft knew no bounds. She endured rigorous training hours learning to sing, dance, and act, honing her skills and pushing herself to new heights. Her innate ability to immerse herself in a role allowed her to breathe life into every character she portrayed, transcending the boundaries of the script and leaving an indelible mark on her audience.

The Gumm Sisters experienced modest success, performing in various local venues in Southern California. However, tragedy struck when their theater burned down in 1935, leaving the family and their dreams in ashes. Undeterred, the resilient Garland and her family relocated to Hollywood, where they believed new opportunities awaited.

In Hollywood, young Garland faced the trials and tribulations that come with pursuing a career in the entertainment industry. She took on odd jobs to support her family, including working at a theater concession stand and even performing singing telegrams. It was during this time that she truly grasped the reality of the industry's challenges. She witnessed the sacrifices required to achieve success, the fickle nature of fame, and the relentless competition that surrounded her.

But amidst the hardships, Garland's talent and dedication soon caught the attention of industry professionals. Her radiant smile, expressive eyes, and undeniable stage presence led to her discovery by famed film producer Louis B. Mayer. Recognizing her potential to become a star, Mayer quickly signed her to a contract with MGM studios, which marked the beginning of her journey towards stardom.

While Garland's career soared to unimaginable heights, her personal life remained complicated. Her relationship with her mother, Ethel, became strained as Ethel assumed the role of her daughter's manager. Ethel pushed her to the limits of her abilities and upheld strict standards that left young Judy feeling overwhelmed and constantly striving for more. The pressure to not only succeed but also to be the family's breadwinner at such a young age took a toll on Garland's mental and emotional well-being.

The early years of Garland's life set the stage for both her successes and struggles in the years to come. The seeds of talent and resilience were sown in her childhood, while the weight of family expectations and personal challenges would shape her tumultuous journey to fame. As Garland ventured further into the world of show business, her early experiences would serve as both a foundation and a source of strength as she reached for the stars.

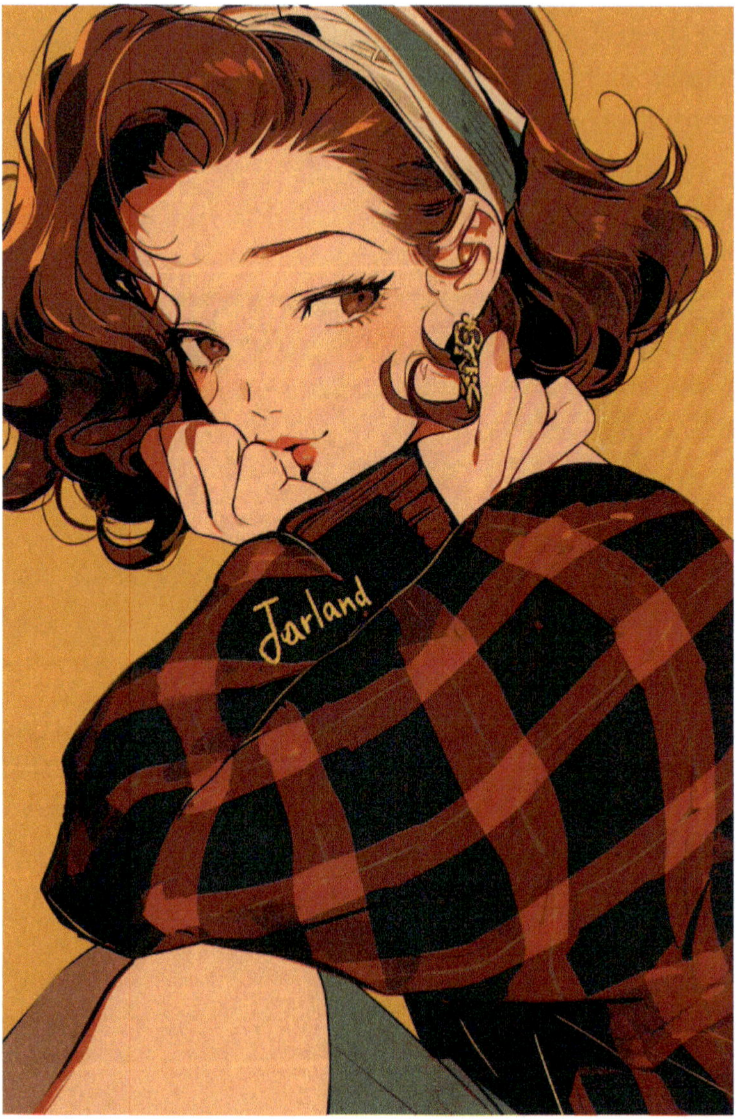
Jarland

chapter 04

Initial steps into show business

Judy Garland's foray into show business began at a very young age, setting the stage for a career that would leave an indelible mark on the entertainment industry. Born Frances Ethel Gumm on June 10, 1922, in Grand Rapids, Minnesota, she exhibited a natural affinity for music and performing from the moment she could speak. Garland's parents, Ethel and Frank Gumm, recognized their daughter's extraordinary talent and decided to nurture her passion, setting in motion a remarkable journey that would shape the course of her life.

At the tender age of two and a half, Garland made her first public appearance at her father Frank's modest movie theater in Lancaster, California. The tiny prodigy, barely able to reach the microphone, belted out "Jingle Bells" with a voice that carried the weight of emotion beyond her years. As she stood on that small stage, expressing joy and exuberance through her heartfelt performance, it became clear to everyone present that they were witnessing the emergence of a true star.

Recognizing the potential within their daughter, Garland's parents sought to refine her talents. They enrolled her in dance classes, where she quickly proved to be a natural. Her grace and mesmerizing presence drew attention wherever she performed, and her parents knew they were nurturing a bona fide talent.

By the age of five, Garland joined her two older sisters, Mary Jane and Dorothy, to form "The Gumm Sisters." With their synchronized dances and harmonious singing, the trio embarked on a series of performances at various vaudeville theaters across California. These early experiences allowed Garland to develop her stage presence and fostered her love for performing. The sisters' dedication to their craft meant that they even continued to perform during tumultuous times, such as when Garland's father tragically passed away in 1935. Their resilience and determination to pursue their dreams despite adversity became a defining characteristic of Garland's career.

Fate intervened serendipitously in 1934 when the Gumm Sisters were signed to a contract with Metro-Goldwyn-Mayer (MGM), one of Hollywood's most prestigious movie studios. Despite the excitement of this opportunity, Mary Jane and Dorothy decided to step away from show business, leaving Frances, now transforming into Judy Garland, to continue her journey solo. It was a pivotal moment in her life, and she embraced the challenge with unyielding determination.

Under the guidance of MGM, Garland began honing her singing, dancing, and acting skills with a dedicated team of coaches. The studio recognized her immense potential and vowed to transform her into a multi-talented entertainer. Her determination to succeed was evident as she embraced each training session with unwavering enthusiasm, learning everything from vocal control to perfecting her dance technique. It was during this period that her distinctive vocal style blossomed, characterized by a unique combination of vulnerability, power, and emotional depth.

In 1936, Garland's talent found its first notable platform when she starred in the short film "Every Sunday" alongside Deanna Durbin, another rising star. The film showcased both Garland's and Durbin's prodigious singing abilities, capturing the hearts of audiences and industry insiders alike. At just fourteen years old, Garland's performance left an indelible impression, foreshadowing the extraordinary career that awaited her.

As Judy Garland continued to flourish as an artist, her star began to ascend within Hollywood's glittering constellation of talent. Renowned figures in the industry took notice of her unmatched talent, mesmerizing stage presence, and tireless work ethic. With each new project, Garland's reputation as a young prodigy grew stronger, as she poured her heart and soul into each role she portrayed.

While Garland's initial steps into show business provided a solid foundation for her extraordinary journey, the road ahead would not be without its challenges and hardships. Facing the pressures of fame, navigating personal struggles, and persevering through demanding work schedules, she would prove time and again that her indomitable spirit and immense talent would triumph over adversity.

From her humble beginnings as a child performer to her early success at MGM, Garland embarked on a path that would lead her to iconic roles, unforgettable performances, and the enduring love and admiration of fans around the world. Little did Judy Garland know at the time that her initial leap into show business would become the catalyst for an unparalleled legacy, transcending generations and continuing to captivate audiences with its timeless magic.

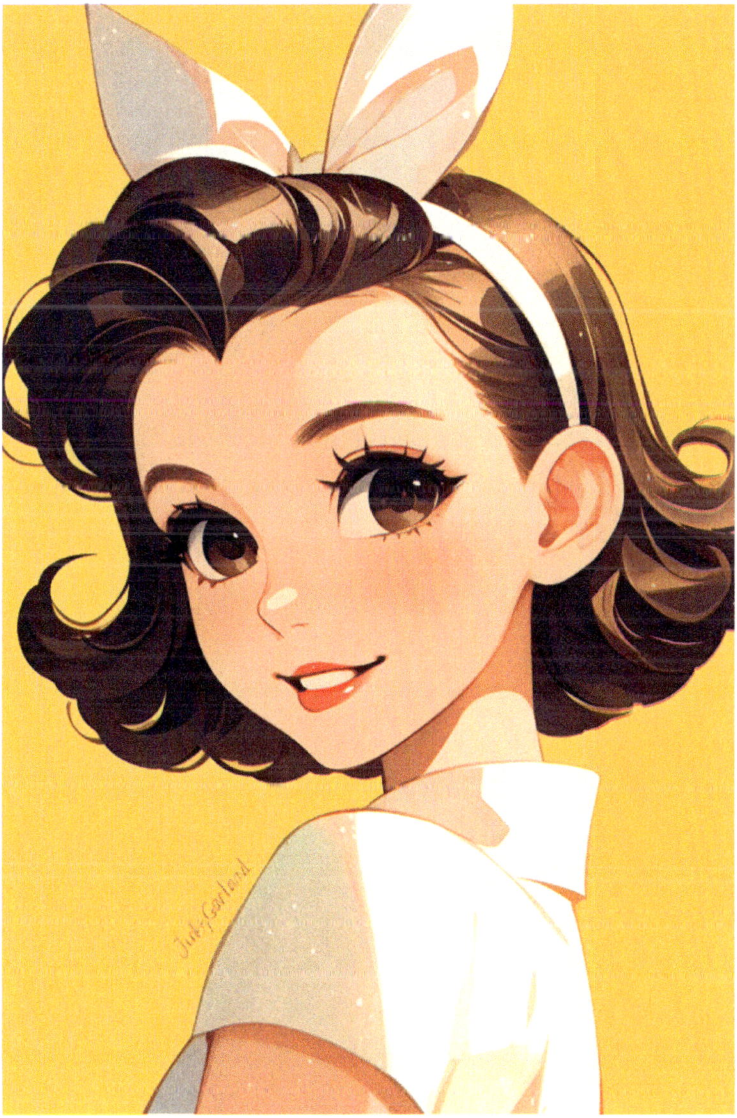
Judy Garland

chapter 05

The transition from Frances Gumm to Judy Garland

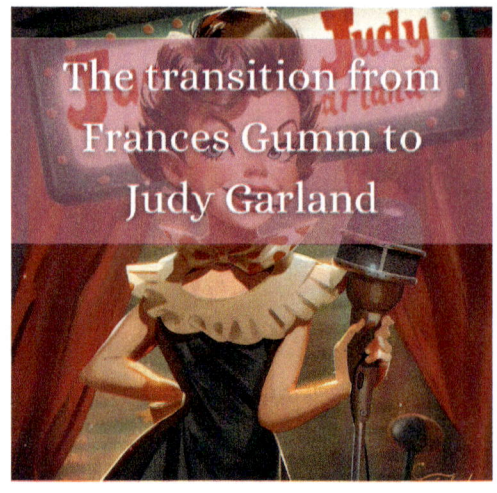

Frances Ethel Gumm was born on June 10, 1922, in Grand Rapids, Minnesota, to Ethel and Frank Gumm. From a young age, Frances showed immense talent and a natural inclination towards performing arts. Aided by her supportive parents, Frances, along with her two older sisters, Virginia and Mary Jane, formed a singing trio known as the "Gumm Sisters." Together, they traversed the Midwest, showcasing their harmonious voices and captivating audiences with their youthful charm.

However, it wasn't until 1934 when Frances Gumm's life would take a significant turn. The family had relocated to California, journeying towards the beckoning lights of Hollywood, hoping to find better opportunities in the entertainment industry. It was during this time that Frances caught the attention of renowned studio executive Louis B. Mayer, whose instrumental role would forever change the trajectory of her career.

Mayer, the head of Metro-Goldwyn-Mayer (MGM) Studios, was immediately struck by Frances' undeniable talent and presence on stage. Recognizing her potential star power, he saw the need for a stage name that would better suit her burgeoning career. Together with MGM's publicity department, they deliberated over numerous options before settling on the name "Judy Garland."

The transition from Frances Gumm to Judy Garland was not just a change in name; it represented a deliberate effort to craft a new persona for the young performer. Garland's new moniker embodied a captivating allure, evoking a sense of timeless appeal and the promise of a captivating talent that transcended age, gender, and time.

Under the meticulous guidance of the MGM studio system, the transformation from Frances to Judy encompassed not just a name change, but also a process of grooming and refinement. Garland underwent extensive vocal training, dance lessons, and acting coaching to further develop her skills and adapt her talent to the demands of the industry.

The alteration of Garland's physical appearance was also a crucial element in the transition. MGM executives believed she needed to be more than just a talented singer; she needed to be a glamorous star. With the expertise of skilled hairstylists, wardrobe departments, and makeup artists, changes were meticulously crafted to enhance Garland's natural beauty and solidify her image as a Hollywood icon.

To ensure her success, MGM organized an extensive publicity campaign to introduce Judy Garland to the world. They carefully controlled her image and managed her public appearances, strategically showcasing her talent and charisma at every opportunity. Garland's transition to Judy unfolded through a carefully choreographed rollout of films, recordings, and live performances, establishing her as a versatile and multi-faceted entertainer.

For Frances Gumm, the transition from an ordinary girl to Judy Garland was both exhilarating and challenging. Although her unparalleled talent remained unchanged, the pressures of fame and the expectations placed upon her were formidable. She had to navigate the complexities of persona management, always portraying herself as the beloved Judy Garland, the girl next door with an extraordinary voice.

As Judy Garland, she captured the hearts of millions with her endearing vulnerability, magnetic stage presence, and incomparable voice. The transition from Frances Gumm to Judy Garland not only propelled her into stardom but also marked the beginning of an illustrious career that would span decades and leave an indelible mark on the world of entertainment.

The transformation from Frances Gumm to Judy Garland encompassed both an artistic evolution and personal growth. Behind the scenes, Garland grappled with the expectations placed upon her, often struggling with self-doubt and the pressures of maintaining her public image. However, she was able to channel her inner strength and resilience into her performances, captivating audiences with her emotionally charged renditions and relatable portrayal of characters.

While the transition from Frances to Judy brought forth new opportunities and recognition, it also meant assuming the role of a cultural icon and bearing the weight of public scrutiny. Garland's journey as Judy Garland was marked by both personal triumphs and tumultuous periods, including battles with mental health issues, strained relationships, and a demanding work schedule.

Despite these challenges, Judy Garland's artistic brilliance continued to shine. Her repertoire expanded beyond singing into acting, winning critical acclaim for her roles in films such as "The Wizard of Oz," "Meet Me in St. Louis," and "A Star is Born." Garland's ability to convey both vulnerability and strength on screen resonated with audiences, affirming her status as one of Hollywood's most celebrated performers.

Beyond her on-screen success, Garland's live performances became legendary. Her concerts were imbued with an electrifying energy, as she poured her heart and soul into every song, captivating audiences with her vocal prowess, sharp comedic timing, and an undeniable connection to the audience. Even in the face of personal struggles, Garland's commitment to her craft and her unwavering dedication to her fans never wavered, leaving an indelible mark on the history of live entertainment.

The transition from Frances Gumm to Judy Garland marked a turning point not only in the life of a young performer but also in the history of entertainment itself. Judy Garland's enduring legacy is a testament to her immense talent, her ability to connect with audiences on a deeply emotional level, and her unwavering commitment to her craft. She remains an icon, inspiring generations of artists to pursue their dreams with passion, resilience, and an unwavering commitment to authenticity.

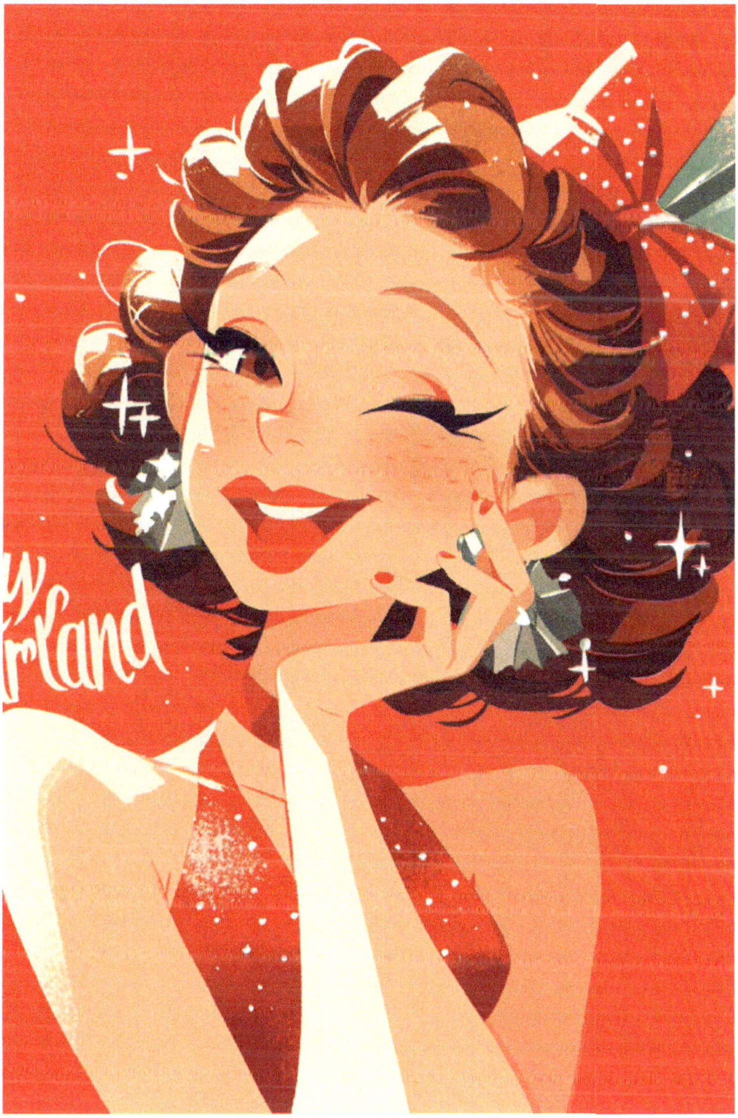

THE JOURNEY TO OZ

chapter 06

Signing with MGM and early roles

Judy Garland's incredible talent and magnetic charisma caught the attention of Louis B. Mayer, the formidable head of Metro-Goldwyn-Mayer (MGM), during one of her captivating performances as a young teen. Mayer, renowned for his keen eye for raw talent and his relentless drive for perfection, immediately recognized Garland's immense potential and wasted no time in signing her to an exclusive contract with the prestigious studio.

Garland's entry into the world of MGM marked the beginning of a transformative period in her life and career. The studio, known for its meticulous grooming of young stars, spared no expense in refining her abilities. Under the watchful eye of Mayer and his team of experts, Garland underwent rigorous training to cultivate her acting, singing, and dancing skills. From vocal lessons to intensive dance classes, every aspect of her performance was meticulously honed to perfection.

MGM recognized that Garland possessed a rare combination of natural talent, vulnerability, and an undeniable charm that set her apart from her peers. Her ethereal voice, filled with emotion and depth, defied her youth and carried an intangible quality that touched the hearts of audiences. Combined with her innate ability to effortlessly convey a wide range of emotions, Garland was destined to become a force to be reckoned with in the realms of both film and music.

Within MGM's well-established studio system, Garland swiftly became part of the studio family. She was not treated as just another actress, but rather as a cherished asset that had the potential to elevate the studio to new heights. Not only did she receive professional training, but she was also carefully molded to fit a specific image that would appeal to audiences worldwide. From selecting her wardrobe to strategizing her public appearances, every aspect of Garland's persona was meticulously crafted to meet the studio's vision of a future leading lady.

In her early MGM films, Garland's roles generally consisted of supporting parts and small performances in musical numbers. While these appearances allowed her to showcase her incredible vocal range and dynamic stage presence, they often took a backseat to the main storylines. Nevertheless, even in these secondary roles, Garland's talent shone through, leaving an indelible mark on audiences.

One notable breakthrough for Garland arrived in 1938 with the film **Listen, Darling**, where she portrayed the young and spirited "Pinkie" alongside Freddie Bartholomew. This heartwarming film showcased Garland's ability to effortlessly convey a range of emotions with authenticity, providing a glimpse into her potential as a leading actress. Drawing upon her own experiences as a teenage girl, Garland brought a level of vulnerability and relatability to Pinkie that resonated deeply with audiences. Her performance in **Listen, Darling** solidified her status as a versatile and gifted performer, earning her critical acclaim and further endearing her to audiences worldwide.

As Garland's star began to ascend at MGM, the studio began offering her more significant roles that allowed her talent to shine in its full glory. In 1939, she starred opposite the charismatic Mickey Rooney in the box office hit **Babes in Arms**. The film, directed by the brilliant Busby Berkeley, served as the perfect vehicle for Garland to showcase her multifaceted abilities. Her portrayal of the young and ambitious Patsy Barton, alongside Rooney's character, epitomized the undeniable chemistry and magnetic energy that the duo shared. Together, they delivered mesmerizing musical numbers that left audiences spellbound. **Babes in Arms** not only cemented Garland as a sought-after performer but also marked the beginning of a legendary partnership with Rooney that would go on to create numerous successful collaborations in the years that followed.

While Garland's film career gained momentum, her live performances also became an integral part of her rising popularity. With her powerful voice and electrifying stage presence, she captivated audiences during vaudeville shows and concert tours across the country. Whether it was performing beloved classics or introducing new songs brimming with raw emotion, Garland's live performances were a testament to her unparalleled talent. The intensity she brought to each note and lyric left concertgoers in awe, often eliciting thunderous applause and tears of joy.

This combination of Garland's film success and live performances further solidified her reputation as an extraordinary entertainer. Fans from all corners of the entertainment world could not help but be captivated, drawn to her vulnerability, authenticity, and a sense of familiarity that resonated deeply with their own experiences. Garland's ability to connect with her audiences on such a profound level propelled her into the realm of superstardom, laying the foundation for a remarkable career that would endure for decades to come.

Signing with MGM opened countless doors for Garland, catapulting her towards a future stardom that few could have predicted. As the young actress transitioned from smaller roles to more significant parts, her undeniable talent and magnetic presence continued to captivate audiences worldwide. Little did anyone know at the time that this extraordinary young woman would transform into one of the most iconic and beloved figures in Hollywood history.

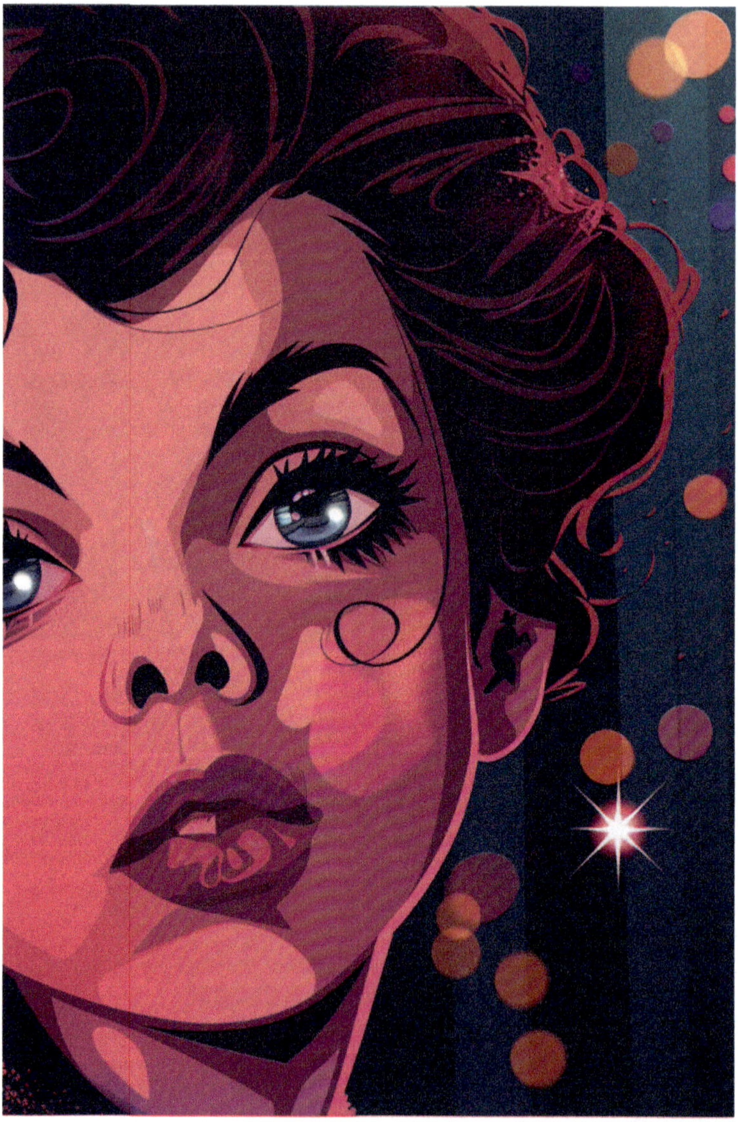

chapter 07

The casting of Dorothy in **The Wizard of Oz**

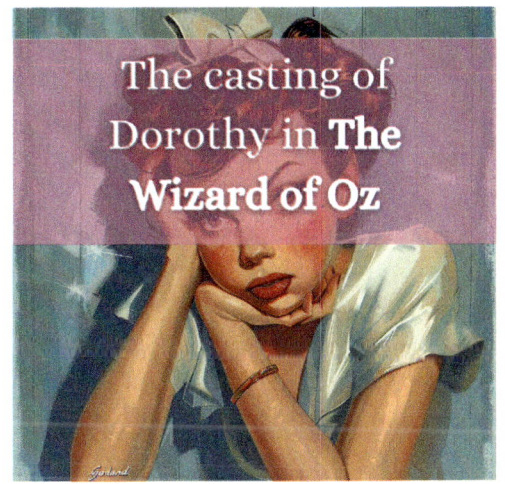

When it came to casting the iconic role of Dorothy in **The Wizard of Oz,** the search was on for a young actress who could capture the innocence, vulnerability, and fierce determination of the character. Judy Garland, then known as Frances Gumm, was just 16 years old when she caught the attention of MGM executives with her exceptional singing abilities and undeniable charm.

Garland's audition for the role of Dorothy was nothing short of magical. As she belted out the heartfelt and longing notes of "Over the Rainbow," it was clear that a star was born. Her performance struck a chord with the casting directors, who recognized the raw talent and emotional depth she brought to the table.

While other actresses were considered for the part, including Shirley Temple and Deanna Durbin, it was Garland's unique combination of innocence, maturity beyond her years, and undeniable talent that ultimately secured her the role. The decision to cast her as Dorothy was a pivotal moment in her career and would forever be associated with her name.

However, the road to becoming Dorothy wasn't without its challenges. Garland faced criticism and skepticism from some within the industry who questioned her suitability for the role. At 16, she was older than the character of Dorothy in L. Frank Baum's book, and there were concerns about her ability to convincingly portray a young girl.

To address these concerns, Garland underwent a physical transformation. Her natural brunette locks were dyed a vibrant shade of Technicolor red, and she wore a specially designed corset to appear more youthful. These changes, along with her undeniable talent, helped sway the skeptics and solidify her as the beloved character of Dorothy.

Beyond her natural talent and physical transformation, Garland's dedication and work ethic played a significant role in her performance as Dorothy. She spent countless hours rehearsing her lines, perfecting her singing, and immersing herself in the character. Garland's commitment to the role paid off, as she seamlessly captured the essence of Dorothy, drawing audiences into her world of wonder and adventure.

However, the pressures of the role and the demanding filming schedule took a toll on Garland's young shoulders. She faced tremendous pressure from the studio and was subjected to grueling working conditions, including long hours on set and strict dieting. These pressures, combined with her own personal insecurities and struggles with mental health, led to a tumultuous period in her life.

Despite the challenges, Garland's performance as Dorothy remains a testament to her immense talent and dedication. The authenticity and emotional depth she brought to the character resonated with audiences worldwide. Her portrayal of Dorothy's longing for a better life, her bravery in the face of uncertainty, and her unwavering belief in the power of dreams touched the hearts of millions.

The significance of Garland's portrayal of Dorothy cannot be overstated. **The Wizard of Oz** remains one of the most beloved and enduring films of all time, and her performance stands as a touchstone for the character. Her heartfelt rendition of "Over the Rainbow" has become an anthem of hope and dreams, resonating with audiences of all ages.

Off-screen, Garland's portrayal of Dorothy had a profound impact on her own life. She became forever intertwined with the character, both praised and burdened by its legacy. The pressures and expectations associated with playing Dorothy would shape her personal and professional journey for years to come.

Garland's performance as Dorothy not only marked a turning point in her career, but it also highlighted her unique ability to connect with audiences on a deeply emotional level. Her portrayal of Dorothy illuminated the universal themes of longing, hope, and the pursuit of happiness. Through her performance, she reminded audiences of the power of imagination and the strength to overcome adversity.

Garland's transformation into Dorothy also reflected the evolving role of women in film at the time. Dorothy was not just a damsel in distress; she was a young girl with agency and independence, willing to fight for what she believed in. Garland's portrayal of Dorothy captured the spirit of a new era, where young women were encouraged to dream big and carve their own paths.

The casting of Judy Garland as Dorothy in **The Wizard of Oz** was a pivotal moment in both her career and the history of cinema. It showcased her immense talent and launched her into superstardom, solidifying her place as one of Hollywood's brightest stars. Her portrayal of Dorothy remains an iconic performance, leaving an indelible mark on the hearts of audiences across generations. It serves as a testament to the enduring power of storytelling and the ability of a single performance to capture the collective imagination.

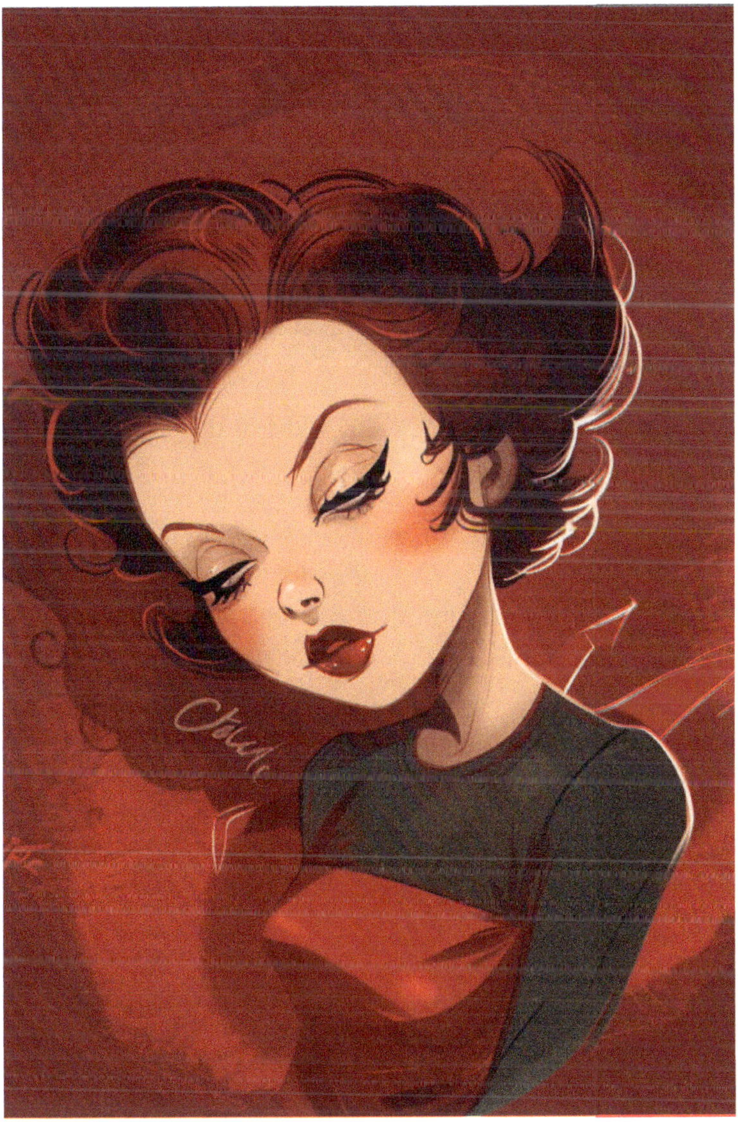

chapter 08

Behind-the-scenes of The Wizard of Oz: Challenges and triumphs

Judy Garland

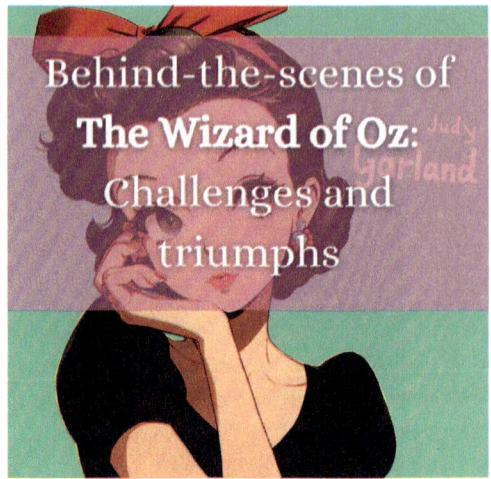

Introduction

The making of **The Wizard of Oz** is a captivating tale filled with numerous challenges and triumphs. Behind-the-scenes, the production encountered a multitude of obstacles that tested the dedication, creativity, and resourcefulness of everyone involved. This extended chapter delves deeper into the behind-the-scenes process, shedding light on the struggles faced and the triumphs achieved that contributed to the creation of one of the greatest films in history.

Creating the Land of Oz

Bringing the magical world of Oz to life was an ambitious and extraordinary endeavor. The vivid and enchanting landscapes depicted in L. Frank Baum's beloved story required meticulous planning and execution. The art directors, including Cedric Gibbons and William Horning, along with the inventive work of production designer Jack Martin Smith, embraced the challenge of constructing the fantastical sets. The Emerald City, with its towering green spires and ethereal glow, was created using a combination of matte paintings, miniatures, and intricate set dressing. The Wicked Witch's castle, designed with gothic elements and draped in darkness, became a menacing backdrop for Dorothy's perilous journey. The attention to detail in every set, from the Munchkinland town square to the haunted apple orchard, contributed to the immersive experience that transported audiences to the Land of Oz.

Costume designer Gilbert Adrian deserves accolades for his remarkable work in bringing the characters to life through their attire. Dorothy's iconic blue gingham dress, often synonymous with the character, symbolized the innocence and purity at the heart of her journey. The Scarecrow, played by Ray Bolger, was adorned in a tattered, straw-stuffed suit that effortlessly conveyed his longing for a brain. The Tin Man, portrayed by Jack Haley, wore a reflective silver suit, intricately designed to give the appearance of a metallic exterior. The Cowardly Lion, embodied by Bert Lahr, donned a shaggy mane, whiskers, and a regal yet comical costume, perfectly capturing his blend of fear and courage. The costume designs became an essential element in defining each character and amplifying the charm and whimsy of the Land of Oz.

Casting Challenges

The process of casting the perfect ensemble for **The Wizard of Oz** was arduous and rife with complexities. Finding an actress who could embody the innocence, courage, and vulnerability of Dorothy proved to be an immense challenge. Judy Garland initially seemed an unlikely choice, as she was deemed too mature for the role. However, when she sang "Over the Rainbow," the vulnerability in her voice and the way she connected emotionally with the lyrics convinced the filmmakers that they had found their Dorothy.

Similarly, casting the beloved characters of the Scarecrow, Tin Man, and Cowardly Lion required careful consideration. Ray Bolger, originally cast as the Tin Man, lobbied for the role of the Scarecrow, believing it suited his physicality and comedic talents better. The filmmakers agreed, resulting in Bolger's iconic portrayal of the floppy, acrobatic Scarecrow.

Buddy Ebsen was initially cast as the Tin Man and completed several weeks of filming before a severe allergic reaction to the aluminum powder used in his makeup forced him to leave the production. Jack Haley stepped in as his replacement, ultimately imbuing the Tin Man with his own unique charm and warmth.

Bert Lahr's interpretation of the Cowardly Lion was rooted in physical comedy and a distinctive voice, making his portrayal unforgettable. Each actor brought their own distinct talents and personalities to their respective roles, enriching the characters and elevating the overall performance of the ensemble.

Technological Innovations

The Wizard of Oz was a pioneer in the use of special effects and innovative filmmaking techniques, pushing the boundaries of cinematic artistry for its time. This section delves deeper into the technical marvels that made the film a visual spectacle. The creation of the tornado scene, for instance, relied on the seamless integration of live-action footage, miniatures, and hand-drawn animation to convey the destructive force of the storm. The special effects team, led by A. Arnold Gillespie, employed a combination of wind machines, debris, and clever editing to create a realistic and awe-inspiring sequence.

Behind Dorothy's memorable arrival in Munchkinland lay the ingenious use of trap doors and overhead rigging. This allowed actors to descend from the ceiling, giving the illusion of characters arriving from the sky. The vibrant transition from the sepia-toned Kansas to the brilliant colors of Oz became a cinematic breakthrough in the use of Technicolor. The cinematographers, Harold Rosson and Ray Rennahan, experimented with different lighting techniques and color gradations to achieve a seamless transformation, further immersing viewers in the magical world on-screen.

The meticulously choreographed dance sequences, such as the iconic "Jitterbug" and the lively celebration in the Emerald City, involved intricate camera movements and precise blocking. The technical team, including choreographer Bobby Connolly and director Victor Fleming, collaborated to capture the energy and vibrancy of these sequences on film.

Despite the limitations of the era's technology, the ingenious use of practical effects, miniatures, animation, and color manipulation allowed **The Wizard of Oz** to transport audiences to a world beyond their wildest imaginings.

Behind-the-Scenes Stories and Anecdotes
Working behind-the-scenes on **The Wizard of Oz** was marked by a rich tapestry of unforgettable stories and anecdotes. From mishaps and unexpected challenges to moments of genius and improvisation, the dedication, creativity, and camaraderie of the cast and crew shone through.

Judy Garland's grueling shooting schedule and the pressures placed on her as a young actress led to her developing a reliance on amphetamines. She battled personal struggles but never let it interfere with her performance, delivering a captivating portrayal of Dorothy that inspired generations.

The production faced numerous challenges, such as working with live animals. The scene in which Dorothy meets the Cowardly Lion required meticulous synchronized movements to ensure the safety of both actors and animals. The steady hand of animal trainer Carl Spitz ensured the successful integration of the live lion and the actors.

Despite facing initial skepticism from studio executives, director Victor Fleming proved instrumental in shaping the final vision of **The Wizard of Oz**. His ability to balance the darker elements of the story with moments of lightheartedness and wonder created a cohesive and engaging narrative.

The friendship that developed between Judy Garland, Ray Bolger, Jack Haley, and Bert Lahr during the production is legendary. They supported one another through the demanding filming schedule, entertained each other with their comedic talents, and formed lasting bonds that extended beyond the set.

The Legacy of The Wizard of Oz

The success of **The Wizard of Oz** extended far beyond its initial release, becoming a timeless classic that continues to captivate audiences to this day. This section takes a closer look at the lasting legacy of the film, exploring how it has permeated popular culture through adaptations, references, and tributes.

Julie Andrews cited **The Wizard of Oz** as her main source of inspiration when preparing for her iconic role in **Mary Poppins**. The influence of **The Wizard of Oz** can also be seen in other notable films, such asOther notable films, such as **The Wiz** (1978), a modern reinterpretation of **The Wizard of Oz** with a predominantly African-American cast, and **Return to Oz** (1985), a darker and more fantastical sequel to the original story.

The Wizard of Oz has also had a significant impact on the world of music. The songs from the film, including "Over the Rainbow," "Follow the Yellow Brick Road," and "We're Off to See the Wizard," have become cultural touchstones and have been covered by countless artists over the years. Judy Garland's rendition of "Over the Rainbow" is widely regarded as one of the greatest movie songs of all time. It won an Academy Award for Best Original Song and has been inducted into the Grammy Hall of Fame.

The influence of **The Wizard of Oz** extends beyond the realms of film and music. The iconic ruby slippers worn by Dorothy have become iconic props in film history. One pair was stolen and remains missing to this day, while several others have been sold at auction for millions of dollars.

In popular culture, references to **The Wizard of Oz** are ubiquitous. From countless parodies and homages in television shows, such as **The Simpsons** and **Family Guy**, to appearances in commercials and advertisements, the film's imagery and characters have permeated various facets of society.

The enduring appeal of **The Wizard of Oz** can be attributed to its timeless themes of self-discovery, friendship, and the power of imagination. The story of Dorothy's journey to find her way back home has resonated with audiences for generations, offering comfort and inspiration to all who watch.

As the film celebrates its 80th anniversary, it continues to be a beloved and cherished piece of cinematic history. The talent and dedication of the cast and crew, coupled with the technical innovations and imaginative storytelling, ensured that **The Wizard of Oz** would stand the test of time and remain an enduring symbol of the magic of cinema.

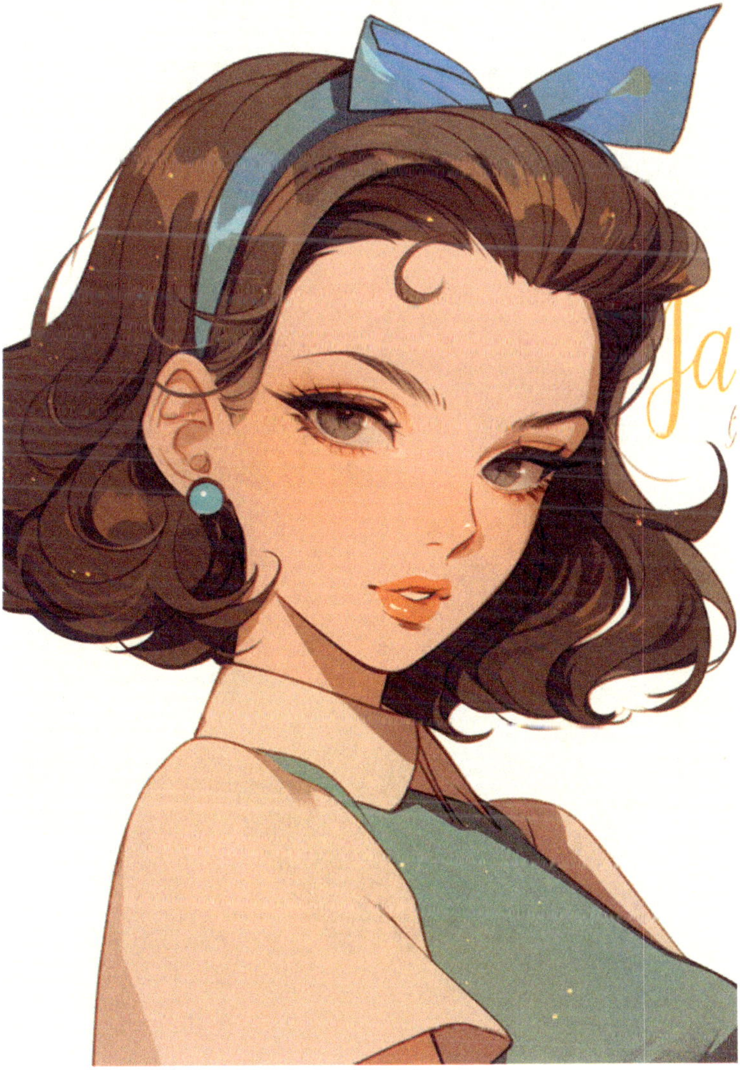

OVER THE RAINBOW

chapter 09

The impact of **The Wizard of Oz** on Garland's career

The release of **The Wizard of Oz** in 1939 marked a pivotal moment in Judy Garland's already promising career. Born Frances Ethel Gumm, Garland had been drawn to perform from a young age, honing her skills in vaudeville alongside her sisters. Her natural talent was evident, and it wasn't long before she caught the attention of industry professionals.

Garland's journey to stardom was not without its challenges. As a young performer, she faced the pressures of being in the spotlight, navigating the demanding world of show business, and facing criticism and rejection. Despite these obstacles, Garland's unwavering dedication to her craft and the unwavering support of her family propelled her forward.

When the opportunity to portray Dorothy Gale in **The Wizard of Oz** presented itself, Garland saw a chance to showcase her abilities and cement her place in the industry. At just sixteen years old, she was tasked with carrying the weight of the film on her young shoulders. The role of Dorothy required a delicate balance of innocence, determination, and vulnerability, and Garland fully embodied the character's essence.

Garland approached the role with a level of maturity beyond her years, pouring her heart and soul into the character. Her expressive eyes and genuine warmth brought Dorothy to life, capturing the hearts of audiences around the world. From the moment she sang "Somewhere Over the Rainbow," it was clear that Garland possessed a rare gift—a voice that could evoke emotions and transport listeners to another world. The emotional depth and purity of her voice resonated, making her performance unforgettable.

The critical and commercial success of **The Wizard of Oz** was overwhelming. Audiences were enchanted by the magical world of Oz, and Garland's portrayal of Dorothy was hailed as one of the finest performances of the era. The film's success not only solidified Garland's status as a Hollywood star but also introduced her exceptional talent to an even wider audience.

Following the triumph of **The Wizard of Oz**, Garland became a household name, celebrated for her undeniable talent. Hollywood recognized her marketability and versatility, leading to a string of successful films and musicals where she had the opportunity to showcase her skills as both an actress and a singer. Despite her young age, she proved herself to be a consummate professional, flawlessly transitioning from lighthearted musicals to more profound and introspective roles.

However, as Garland's career progressed, she faced challenges in breaking away from the shadow of Dorothy Gale. The public's perception of her was often intrinsically linked to the image of the young girl from Kansas, which led to her being typecast and limited in the range of roles she was offered. Though frustrating, Garland used her determination and resilience to push against these constraints, determined to prove herself as a multifaceted performer capable of much more.

One notable film that showcased Garland's growth as both an actress and a singer was **Meet Me in St. Louis** (1944). In this beloved musical, she portrayed Esther Smith, a character who showcased Garland's ability to convey a wide range of emotions. From the innocence of "The Trolley Song" to the melancholic longing of "Have Yourself a Merry Little Christmas," Garland's performances were nothing short of mesmerizing. Her nuanced portrayal of Esther Smith revealed a depth and maturity that resonated with audiences and garnered critical acclaim.

Another striking film in Garland's post-**Wizard of Oz** career was **A Star is Born** (1954). In this dramatic musical, she played the role of Vicki Lester, a rising star grappling with fame's pitfalls. The film allowed Garland to explore the complexities of stardom and the toll it takes on one's personal life. Her portrayal of Vicki Lester demonstrated her maturity as an actress, balancing vulnerability, strength, and artistic prowess. Although she didn't win the Academy Award for her performance, many consider her performance in **A Star is Born** as one of her most remarkable achievements.

In addition to her film work, Garland's live performances and recordings showcased her unmatched talent and ability to connect with audiences on a deeply emotional level. Her live concerts were transformative experiences, with her powerful voice filling the room and effortlessly captivating all who listened. Songs like "Get Happy" and "The Man That Got Away" solidified her reputation as one of the greatest vocalists of her time, and her live performances, including her iconic concerts at Carnegie Hall, further cemented her legacy as an extraordinary artist.

It's important to recognize that Garland's success extended beyond the immediate acclaim of her post-**Wizard of Oz** films. The enduring popularity of **The Wizard of Oz** introduced new generations to her work, ensuring the recognition of her unparalleled talent and the impact she had on the entertainment industry. Garland's contributions to music and film continue to be celebrated, and her influence can be observed in the countless performers who followed in her footsteps.

In conclusion, **The Wizard of Oz** played a transformative role in Judy Garland's career, catapulting her to stardom and setting her on a path towards becoming a Hollywood legend. While it initially led to typecasting, it also provided her with a platform to showcase her extraordinary talents. Garland's unwavering dedication to her craft and her ability to authentically connect with audiences are what made her stand out among her peers. Beyond the immediate impact, **The Wizard of Oz** continues to captivate audiences and pay tribute to Garland's remarkable abilities as both a performer and an artist.

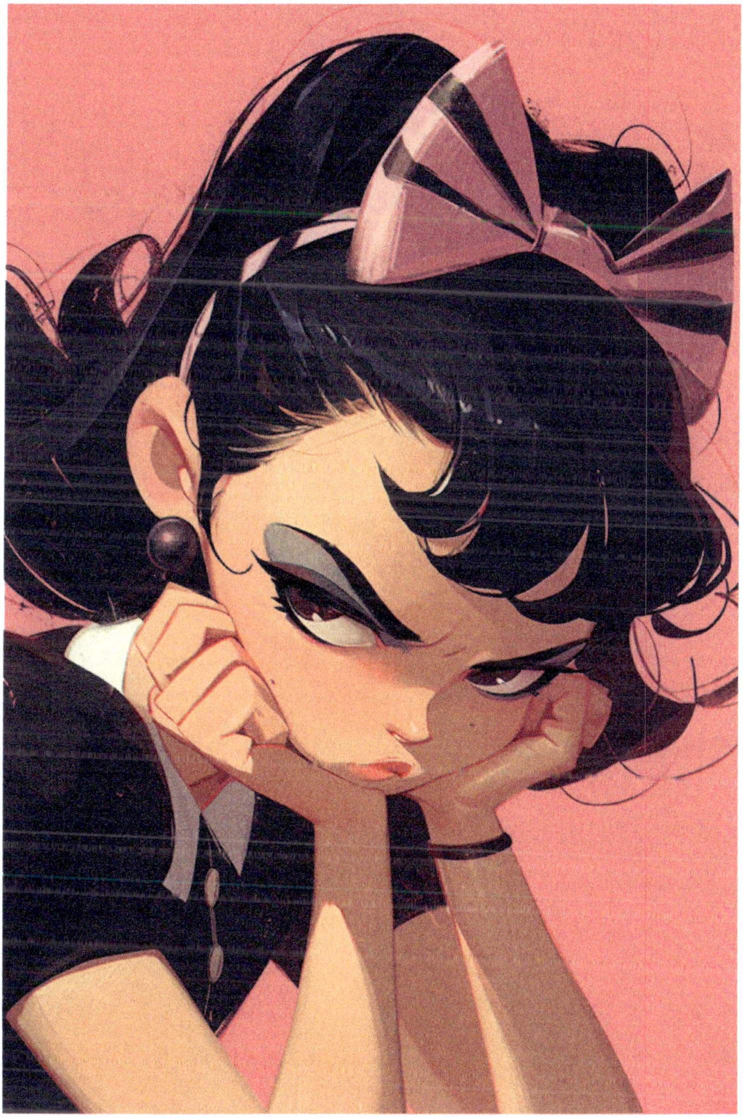

chapter 10

Critical and public reception of the film and Garland's performance

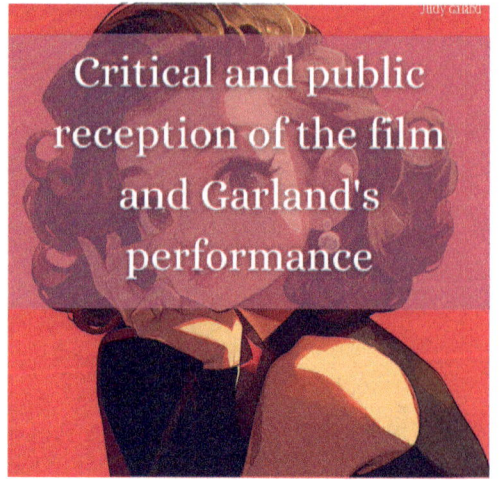

The release of "The Wizard of Oz" in 1939 catapulted Judy Garland into unprecedented stardom and forever changed the course of her career. This chapter explores the critical and public reception of the film and Garland's performance as Dorothy.

Upon its release, "The Wizard of Oz" received mixed reviews from critics, reflecting the diverse opinions on its artistic merits and departure from L. Frank Baum's original book. Some praised the film's imaginative storytelling, breathtaking visuals, and innovative use of Technicolor. They applauded the film's ability to transport viewers to the enchanting world of Oz and hailed it as a landmark achievement in cinematic artistry. These critics admired the film's embodiment of fantasy and escapism, seeing it as a necessary respite from the harsh realities of the Great Depression and looming global conflict.

Others, however, lamented its deviations from the source material, expressing disappointment in the liberties taken with the story. They argued that the film sacrificed some of the book's subtleties and character development in favor of spectacle and entertainment. The inclusion of musical numbers, while beloved by many, proved divisive. Some critics felt that the songs disrupted the flow of the narrative and were unnecessary distractions.

Amidst these contrasting opinions, one aspect of the film remained universally acclaimed: Judy Garland's performance as Dorothy. At just sixteen years old, Garland brought a vulnerability and sincerity to the role that resonated deeply with audiences around the world. Her portrayal of Dorothy, a young girl longing for adventure and a place to call home, struck a chord with viewers of all ages. Garland's ability to convey genuine emotions, be it fear, joy, or determination, captivated audiences and made Dorothy someone they could connect with on a visceral level.

Garland's powerful rendition of the iconic song "Over the Rainbow" became a defining moment in cinematic history, encapsulating the hopes and dreams of millions during a time of uncertainty. The song's message of longing for something more spoke to people's desires for a brighter future or a place where they felt accepted and understood. It became an anthem for anyone who dared to dream beyond their current circumstances and inspired generations to believe in the power of hope.

The public response to Garland's performance was overwhelming and effusive. Audiences were enraptured by her innocence, charm, and undeniable talent. Garland's portrayal of Dorothy not only endeared her to fans but also showcased her ability to infuse emotional depth into her performances. Her chemistry with the lovable characters she encounters on her journey, such as the Scarecrow, Tin Man, and Cowardly Lion, added to the film's enchanting appeal, creating a sense of camaraderie and friendship for the audience.

"The Wizard of Oz" quickly became a box-office sensation, surpassing all expectations and establishing itself as a beloved classic. Garland's portrayal of Dorothy played a significant role in the film's enduring popularity. She brought an authenticity to the character that made Dorothy relatable and endearing, allowing audiences to empathize with her quest to find her way back home. Dorothy's longing for belonging and her unwavering determination resonated with viewers, reminding them of their own dreams and struggles.

In addition to the film's commercial success, Garland's performance garnered widespread critical acclaim. Many reviewers marveled at her ability to convey a range of emotions, from fear and confusion to determination and resilience. They praised her natural talent for acting, singing, and dancing, recognizing her as a rare and extraordinary talent in the industry. Garland's portrayal of Dorothy was applauded for its nuanced portrayal of adolescence, capturing the essence of both innocence and strength as she navigates the challenges of an unfamiliar world.

"The Wizard of Oz" not only solidified Garland's status as a remarkable actress and singer but also showcased her versatility. While the film was primarily seen as a family-friendly fantasy, Garland's performance transcended the genre, appealing to audiences of all ages and resonating with them on a deeper emotional level. Her portrayal of Dorothy became an embodiment of hope, resilience, and the universal desire for a place to call home.

The impact of "The Wizard of Oz" on Garland's career cannot be overstated. It marked the beginning of a remarkable journey for the young talent who would go on to leave an indelible mark on the world of entertainment. The critical and public reception of the film and Garland's performance solidified her status as an icon of the silver screen and set the stage for her future successes.

In the next chapter, we will delve deeper into Garland's career after "The Wizard of Oz" and explore the films and performances that further cemented her place in Hollywood history, showcasing her as more than just Dorothy Gale but as a versatile and timeless talent.

Judy Garland

chapter 11

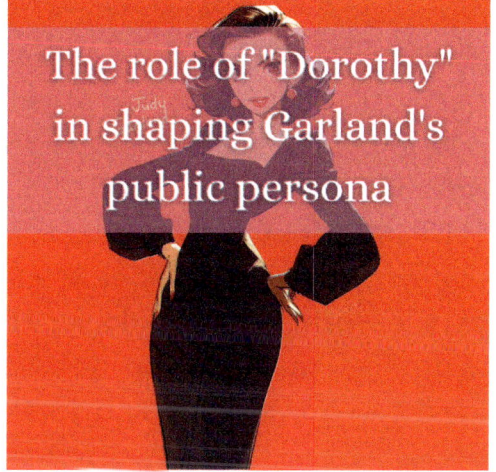

The role of "Dorothy" in shaping Judy Garland's public persona

From the moment Judy Garland stepped into the ruby slippers of Dorothy Gale in "The Wizard of Oz," her life would be forever changed. As the young girl from Kansas, Garland captivated audiences and etched herself into the hearts of millions around the world. But it wasn't just the character of Dorothy that endeared Garland to the public; it was the depth and vulnerability she brought to the role that shaped her public persona.

Playing Dorothy required Garland to tap into a range of emotions, from innocence and wonder to bravery and determination. Through her portrayal, Garland captured the essence of a relatable and aspirational character that resonated with viewers of all ages. As Dorothy faced adversity and explored the strange and magical world of Oz, Garland's genuine performance allowed audiences to connect with her on a deeply emotional level.

At the heart of Dorothy's journey was her longing for home, her yearning for a place where she felt safe, loved, and understood. Garland's own tumultuous childhood contributed to her understanding of this desire and her ability to convey it on screen. Born Frances Ethel Gumm, Garland faced numerous challenges from an early age, including a demanding stage mother, the pressure of early stardom, and a constant battle with insecurity and self-doubt. These experiences, both painful and transformative, echoed through the character of Dorothy, adding an extra layer of authenticity to Garland's portrayal.

While portraying Dorothy, Garland showcased her magnetic screen presence and undeniable talent. Her singing voice soared through songs like "Over the Rainbow" with such raw emotion that it became an anthem of hope and dreams for a generation. People saw themselves in Dorothy, and in turn, saw themselves in Judy Garland. She became a symbol of strength, perseverance, and the power of dreams.

Off-screen, Garland's own struggles and personal challenges added another layer of complexity to her public persona. As she encountered setbacks and faced adversity in her personal life, people couldn't help but draw parallels between Garland and Dorothy. Just as Dorothy faced the Wicked Witch and the challenges of her journey, Garland battled her own demons and navigated the ups and downs of fame and fortune.

Behind the scenes, Garland often faced immense pressure from the studio system. She was subjected to strict diets, amphetamines to control her weight, and relentless work schedules that left her physically and emotionally drained. These experiences further shaped her public image, making her relatable to those who saw her as a symbol of resilience in the face of adversity.

However, the impact of Dorothy on Garland's public persona extended beyond her role in "The Wizard of Oz." It influenced her subsequent career in unforeseen ways. Directors and studios began to recognize and capitalize on her ability to tap into the emotions of a character and elicit genuine empathy from audiences. This led to more complex and nuanced roles, allowing Garland to showcase her range as an actress beyond the beloved character of Dorothy.

By the time she played Dorothy, Garland had already been acting for over a decade, starting her career as a child star. However, it was the role of Dorothy that solidified her status as a true Hollywood legend. The success of "The Wizard of Oz" elevated her to new heights, and Garland took on a newfound responsibility. She became a role model for young fans and an inspiration to aspiring actors and singers around the world.

But along with the positive impact of Dorothy on Garland's public persona, there were also challenges. Being forever associated with one iconic role had its drawbacks, as it created expectations and pigeonholed Garland in the eyes of some critics and industry professionals. They questioned whether she could ever escape the shadow of Dorothy to establish herself as a versatile and profound actress.

Despite these challenges, Garland's talent and dedication to her craft ensured that she would leave an indelible mark on the industry and continue to captivate audiences long after her time in the ruby slippers. She went on to deliver memorable performances in films like "Meet Me in St. Louis," "A Star is Born," and "Judgment at Nuremberg." Each role showcased her versatility and depth as an actress, proving that she was much more than just the girl from Kansas.

In conclusion, the role of Dorothy in "The Wizard of Oz" played a crucial role in shaping Judy Garland's public persona. Through her heartfelt portrayal, she became more than just an actress; she became a symbol of hope, perseverance, and the power of dreams. While the character of Dorothy may have been Garland's most famous role, it was her ability to bring depth and vulnerability to the screen that solidified her status as a timeless Hollywood legend.

Beyond the iconic portrayal, Garland's personal experiences and struggles added depth to her performance, making Dorothy a reflection of her own journey as well as a source of inspiration for audiences worldwide. As Dorothy, Garland became a beacon of hope and a reminder that even in the face of adversity, one can find the strength to persevere. Her legacy will forever be intertwined with the iconic character of Dorothy, a testament to her talent, resilience, and everlasting impact on the world of entertainment.

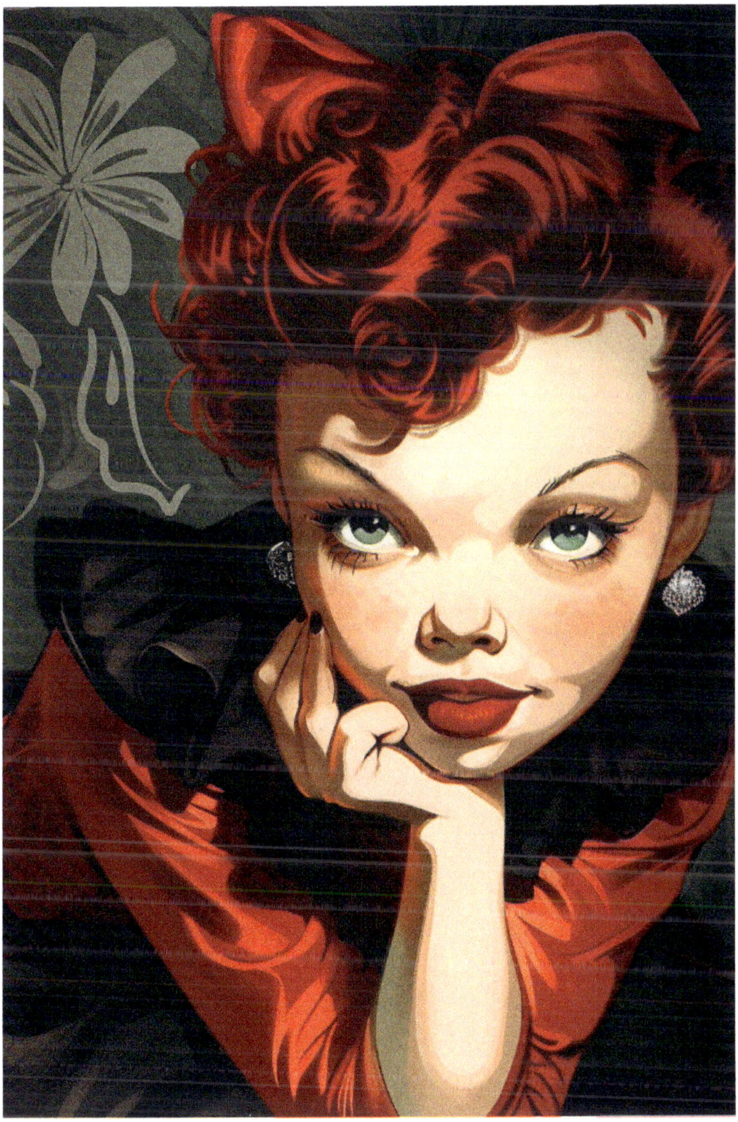

BEYOND OZ: THE GOLDEN YEARS

chapter 12

Key movies and performances post-Oz

After the extraordinary success of "The Wizard of Oz," Judy Garland's career skyrocketed, catapulting her into the stratosphere of stardom and transforming her into one of Hollywood's most sought-after talents. Her next projects not only further showcased her tremendous talent but also solidified her status as a true icon of the silver screen.

One of Garland's most notable post-Oz films was "Meet Me in St. Louis" (1944), directed by the visionary Vincente Minnelli, who would later become her husband. This heartwarming musical set during the 1904 World's Fair introduced Garland as Esther Smith, the second eldest daughter of the Smith family. In this role, she captivated audiences with her radiant charm and unforgettable rendition of the classic song "Have Yourself a Merry Little Christmas." Garland's portrayal of Esther showcased her natural ability to connect with viewers on an emotional level. Her performance, filled with innocence and sincerity, resonated deeply, solidifying her reputation as a consummate performer capable of capturing the hearts of audiences worldwide.

Another standout film in Garland's post-Oz career was "A Star is Born" (1954), a romantic drama musical directed by the legendary George Cukor. In this mesmerizing film, Garland portrayed two characters: Esther Blodgett, an aspiring singer, and Vicki Lester, the persona she adopts as her star rises while her husband, played by James Mason, battles his own demons. Garland's performance as Esther showcased her dramatic prowess, allowing her to explore a complex and intense role in which she seamlessly merged vulnerability and strength. Her character's journey from humble beginnings to becoming a renowned star resonated deeply with audiences, who were captivated by Garland's ability to convey raw emotion on screen. In a career filled with unforgettable musical performances, her rendition of the film's show-stopping number, "The Man That Got Away," remains one of her most iconic and revered musical moments.

Garland also delved into the realm of comedy with films like "The Harvey Girls" (1946), directed by George Sidney. This lively and enchanting musical, set in the 1880s, centers around Susan Bradley, portrayed by Garland, who joins a group of waitresses known as the Harvey Girls. Garland's infectious energy and dazzling musical numbers, including the Academy Award-winning song "On the Atchison, Topeka and the Santa Fe," added a touch of magic to the film. Her impeccable comedic timing, paired with her undeniable charm, created moments of pure joy for moviegoers, further cementing her versatility as an actress.

In addition to her remarkable film work, Garland's live performances became legendary in their own right. Notably, her historic concerts at the Palace Theatre in New York City in 1951 broke records and left audiences in awe. These performances, often referred to as a milestone in her career, showcased Garland's incomparable voice and magnetic stage presence. Every note she sang seemed to come from the depths of her soul, and every emotional beat she delivered resonated with the audience in a profound manner. She effortlessly commanded the stage, captivating audiences with her heartfelt performances and leaving an indelible impression that lingered long after the final encore.

Garland's post-Oz movies and live performances not only highlighted her unparalleled ability to captivate audiences but also revealed the remarkable depth of her talent. Despite the personal and professional challenges she faced, from the relentless pressures of Hollywood to the weight of expectations and her tumultuous personal life, Garland remained unwavering in her commitment to her craft. With every performance, she poured her heart and soul into her work, creating moments of pure magic that will forever be etched in the annals of entertainment history.

Through her post-Oz career, Judy Garland left an indelible mark on the world of film and performance. Her immense talent, combined with her extraordinary ability to connect with audiences on an emotional level, solidified her status as one of the greatest performers of all time. Garland's legacy continues to inspire generations of artists and continues to shine brightly in the hearts of her admirers around the world.

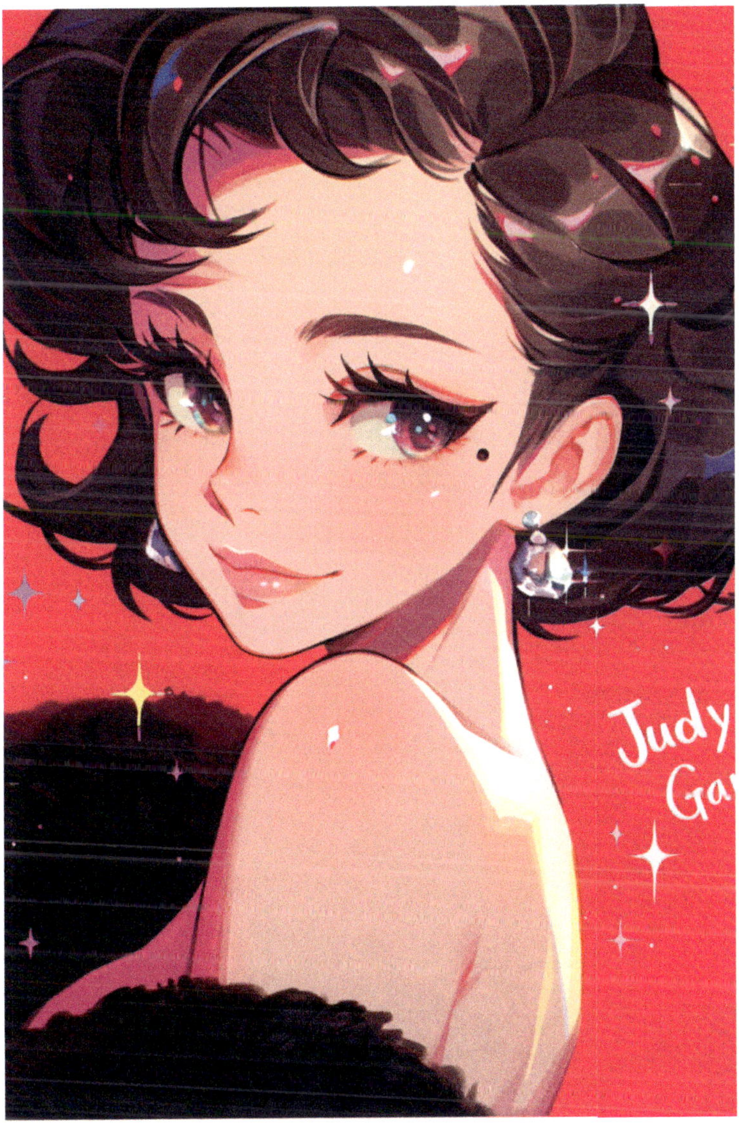
Judy
Ga

chapter 13

Collaborations with notable directors and actors

Throughout her illustrious career, Judy Garland had the opportunity to collaborate with some of the most talented directors and actors in Hollywood. These partnerships not only elevated her performances but also showcased her versatility and range as an actress, leaving an indelible mark on the history of cinema.

One of Garland's most iconic collaborations was with director Vincente Minnelli, whom she married in 1945. Their creative partnership extended beyond their personal relationship and resulted in several critically acclaimed films. In 1944, Minnelli directed Garland in the musical film "Meet Me in St. Louis," based on the stories by Sally Benson. This film not only showcased Garland's acting and singing abilities but also marked a significant departure from the traditional musicals of the time. Minnelli's meticulous attention to detail, visually stunning set designs, and emphasis on character development allowed Garland to fully immerse herself in the role of Esther Smith, a memorable character with depth and relatability. The film became a classic, and Garland's rendition of "Have Yourself a Merry Little Christmas" has since become synonymous with the holiday season. Their artistic collaboration continued with films like "The Clock" (1945) and "The Pirate" (1948), further solidifying their status as a dynamic creative duo.

Garland's collaboration with director George Cukor also played a pivotal role in her career. In 1954, they worked together on the beloved musical "A Star is Born," a remake of the original film from 1937. Cukor's directorial finesse and ability to capture emotional nuance brought out the best in Garland's performance. The film follows the rise of Esther Blodgett, played by Garland, an aspiring singer who gets noticed by a famous actor while performing at a nightclub. Cukor's guidance allowed Garland to delve deep into the emotional complexities of her character, capturing both her vulnerability and strength. This film marked a significant turning point in her career, as it showcased her dramatic abilities alongside her singing talent. Garland's portrayal of Esther Blodgett had a rawness and vulnerability that resonated with audiences, making them empathize with her character's journey. Her powerful and heartfelt performance in the film earned her an Academy Award nomination for Best Actress, solidifying her as one of Hollywood's leading talents.

Another notable collaboration took place between Garland and director Arthur Freed on the film "Easter Parade" in 1948. As one of the significant musicals of the era, this film allowed Garland to showcase her chemistry and exceptional dancing skills alongside the legendary Fred Astaire. Freed, known for his work as a producer and songwriter, brought his expertise to the project, working closely with director Charles Walters. Under Freed's production and Walters' direction, their partnership resulted in captivating dance numbers and memorable musical performances. The film's success was attributed not only to the undeniable talent of its leading actors but also to Freed's imaginative choreography and ability to create magical visual spectacles. With Garland's effervescent presence and Astaire's graceful moves, the film continues to charm audiences to this day, further solidifying Garland's reputation as an extraordinary entertainer.

In addition to working with renowned directors, Garland had the opportunity to share the screen with some of Hollywood's most talented actors. One notable collaboration was with Mickey Rooney, with whom she appeared in a total of nine films. Rooney's energy and comedic timing complemented Garland's own vivacity, creating a dynamic duo that captivated audiences of the time. Their partnership began in their teenage years, with films like "Thoroughbreds Don't Cry" (1937) and "Andy Hardy Meets Debutante" (1940). These films showcased their youthful exuberance and undeniable talents, capturing the spirit of the times and garnering a tremendous following. Together, they portrayed a genuine and heartwarming camaraderie that resonated with audiences and endeared them to millions.

Another memorable collaboration for Garland was with actor James Mason in "A Star is Born." Mason's commanding presence and nuanced portrayal of Norman Maine countered Garland's vulnerability, creating a deeply emotional connection. The film explores the pitfalls of fame and the sacrifices one makes in the pursuit of their dreams. Mason's ability to navigate between emotional intensity and vulnerability provided the perfect foil for Garland's nuanced portrayal of Esther Blodgett's transformation into a star. Their collaboration not only showcased their exceptional acting capabilities but also immortalized "A Star is Born" as one of Hollywood's greatest classics.

Garland's collaborations with directors and actors not only brought out the best in her performances but also contributed to the enduring legacy of her work. These partnerships helped showcase Garland's immense talent, versatility, and ability to connect with audiences on an emotional level. Behind the scenes, the relationships she formed with these notable figures played a significant role in shaping her artistic growth and personal development. The innovative directing styles of Minnelli, Cukor, and Freed, along with the extraordinary acting talents of Mason, Rooney, and Astaire, pushed Garland to explore new depths, breaking boundaries and setting new standards in the world of entertainment.

Through their combined efforts, these collaborations immortalized Garland's talent and solidified her status as a Hollywood legend. Their films continue to captivate and inspire audiences of all generations, reminding us of the enduring power of the silver screen and the magic created by the collaboration between exceptional artists.

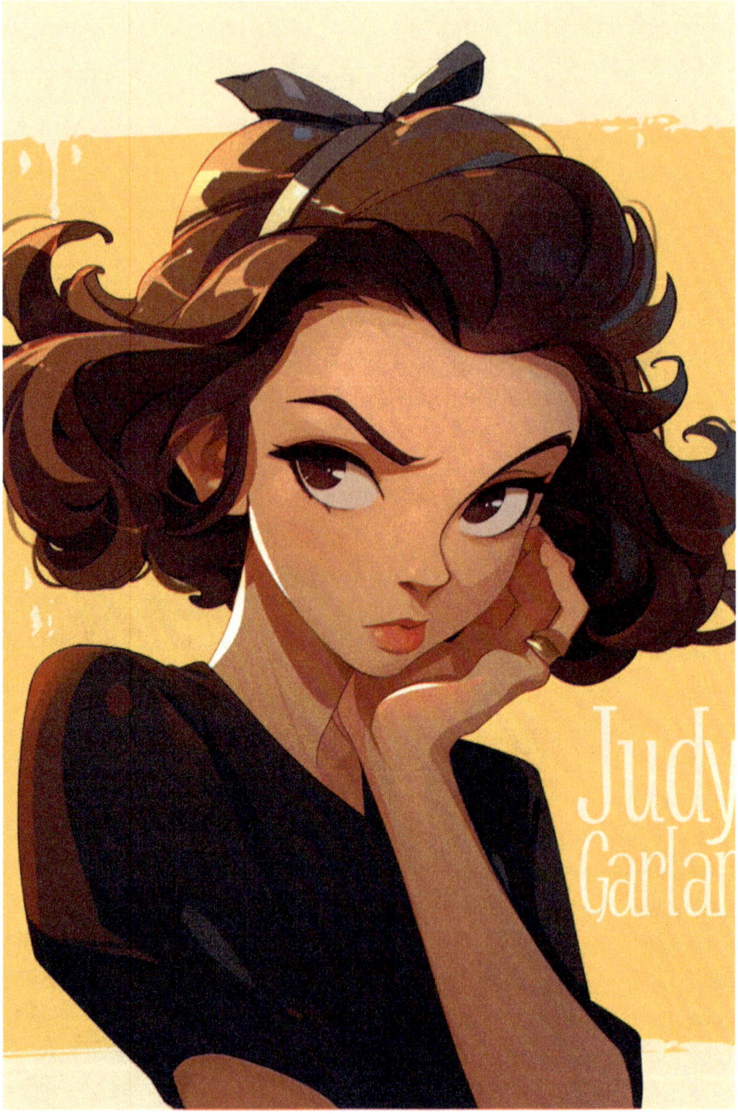
Judy
Garlan

chapter 14

The evolution of Garland's acting and singing style

Throughout her illustrious career, which spanned several decades, Judy Garland continuously showcased a remarkable evolution in both her acting and singing style. From her early years as a child star to her later performances as a mature artist, Garland's journey of growth and adaptability as an entertainer left an indelible mark on the world of cinema and music.

In her early years, Garland's acting style was marked by an effortless charm and a vulnerability that captivated audiences. As a child prodigy, she possessed an innate ability to connect with viewers from the screen, conveying a wide range of emotions with authenticity and sincerity. Her breakthrough role as Dorothy in "The Wizard of Oz" exemplified this natural talent, as she effortlessly transported audiences into the fantastical world of Oz, touching their hearts with her portrayal of a young girl in search of home.

As Garland matured and experienced life's joys and sorrows, her acting style evolved into one that encompassed greater depth and complexity. She began to delve into more challenging roles that showcased the full spectrum of human emotion. In films like "The Clock" and "A Star is Born," Garland portrayed characters who grappled with the complexities of love, ambition, and personal struggles.

In "The Clock," Garland's character Alice Mayberry, a young woman who falls in love with a soldier on leave during World War II, showcased the growth of her acting prowess. The role required her to convey the blossoming of love, the anxieties of separation, and the resilience of the human spirit during a time of great uncertainty. Garland imbued Alice with a tender vulnerability, capturing the hopes and fears of the era, as well as giving voice to the yearnings of audiences watching the film.

In "A Star is Born," perhaps one of Garland's most iconic roles, she portrayed Esther Blodgett, a young woman with dreams of becoming a star in the ruthless world of Hollywood. Garland's performance was a tour de force, as she showcased a range of emotions, from the euphoria of success to the soul-crushing despair of personal tragedy. Her ability to embody the complexities of ambition, vulnerability, and self-discovery made her portrayal of Esther a defining moment in her career, and a reflection of her own personal struggles and triumphs.

Parallel to her acting growth, Garland's singing style underwent a remarkable transformation throughout her career. While she initially enchanted listeners with her sweet and pure voice as a child star, she ultimately emerged as a powerhouse vocalist, capable of delivering performances that defied all expectations. Garland's voice matured into a rich, velvety instrument, resonating with a soul-stirring intensity.

In her later years, Garland's voice took on a depth and gravitas that could only come from a lifetime of experiences. Her renditions of timeless classics like "Over The Rainbow" and "The Man That Got Away" became iconic, as she imbued each lyric with an emotional gravitas that seemed to effortlessly transport listeners into her world.

Garland's singing style was characterized by her distinctive phrasing, impeccable timing, and an innate knack for storytelling through song. She possessed an unparalleled ability to infuse her vocals with raw emotion, allowing her to connect deeply with both the lyrics and the melodies. This unique talent enabled her to deliver performances that were transformative experiences, whetting the appetite of audiences who craved the expressive power of her voice.

In addition to her natural talent, Garland's unwavering dedication to her craft played a pivotal role in the evolution of her acting and singing style. She pushed herself, seeking opportunities to challenge her abilities and expand her artistic horizons. Whether she was tackling complex roles that demanded emotional depth or experimenting with different musical genres, Garland fearlessly embraced the unknown, always striving to connect with her audience on a deeper level.

Her commitment to her craft was evident in her rigorous rehearsal schedules and her willingness to experiment with new vocal techniques and acting methods. Garland tirelessly honed her skills, constantly refining her performances to ensure that she delivered nothing less than her absolute best.

Ultimately, the evolution of Garland's acting and singing style was a testament to her incredible talent, relentless determination, and her unwavering passion for her craft. She left an indelible legacy as a versatile and influential entertainer, inspiring generations of actors and singers to embrace their own artistic growth and push the boundaries of their abilities. Garland's ability to captivate and move audiences through her performances serves as a timeless reminder of the transformative power of the performing arts.

chatvariety.com

A STAR'S STRUGGLE

chapter 15

Personal challenges: Marriage, health, and addiction

Judy Garland's life was marked by a series of personal struggles that extended beyond what the public eye could see. As her career blossomed, so did the challenges in her personal life, including difficulties within her marriages, ongoing health issues, and battles with addiction.

Garland's first marriage to composer David Rose in 1941 was seemingly a fairytale romance. The couple eloped after a whirlwind courtship, but their union soon began to unravel. Garland's demanding schedule as a rising star and Rose's own career commitments resulted in little time together. The distance, both physical and emotional, further isolated Garland, nurturing feelings of insecurity and loneliness. Her relentless touring and the pressures of being in the public eye took a toll on their marriage, exacerbating Garland's mental health issues, including anxiety and depression. These challenges, coupled with Garland's increasing reliance on prescription medications, ultimately led to their divorce in 1944, after three years of struggling to maintain a stable relationship.

Following the end of her marriage to Rose, Garland embarked on a series of failed relationships and marriages. She married director Vincente Minnelli in 1945, giving birth to their daughter, Liza Minnelli. On the surface, the couple appeared to be well-suited, with both heavily involved in the entertainment industry. However, behind closed doors, their marriage faced its own set of trials. Garland's grueling work schedule and the unrelenting pressure to maintain her status as a performer often overshadowed their relationship. Minnelli's own career demands frequently led to prolonged periods of separation, further straining the marriage. Garland's mental and emotional struggles, amplified by Minnelli's controlling nature, and her escalating issues with substance abuse contributed to their divorce in 1951, after six years of marriage.

Throughout her career, Garland's health issues significantly impacted not only her personal life but also her ability to navigate the demands of her profession. She battled chronic fatigue, recurring respiratory problems, and hormonal imbalances. The combination of her strenuous work schedule, the pressure to maintain her petite figure, and frequent dieting took a toll on her well-being. Garland turned to amphetamines and barbiturates in an attempt to manage her weight and boost her energy levels, unintentionally descending into a dangerous cycle of dependency that haunted her for years to come.

The pressures of Hollywood and the entertainment industry further exacerbated Garland's addiction issues. The relentless expectation to maintain a certain image, alongside continuous scrutiny from the media, created a toxic environment for her mental and emotional well-being. Seeking solace and relief from the stress and anxieties that plagued her personal and professional life, Garland found solace in drug use, unknowingly spiraling into a treacherous path of addiction that overshadowed her talent and success.

The consequences of her addiction prompted Garland to seek help through various rehab and treatment programs. However, the grip of her substance abuse proved difficult to shake, resurfacing at multiple points in her life. Her battles with addiction strained her relationships, particularly with her children, who witnessed the devastating effects it had on their beloved mother, creating lasting emotional scars.

Despite her ongoing struggles, Garland's talent and resilience remained. Even amid her personal hardships, she possessed a unique ability to captivate audiences with her rich, emotionally-charged voice and vulnerable performances. Her artistry provided a refuge, a means of expression that allowed her to connect with others on a deep and profound level.

In the next chapter, we will delve into the professional setbacks and comebacks that shaped Garland's career, unveiling her unwavering determination to create art despite the immense personal challenges she faced.

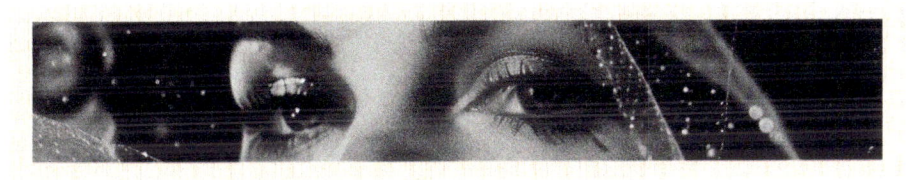

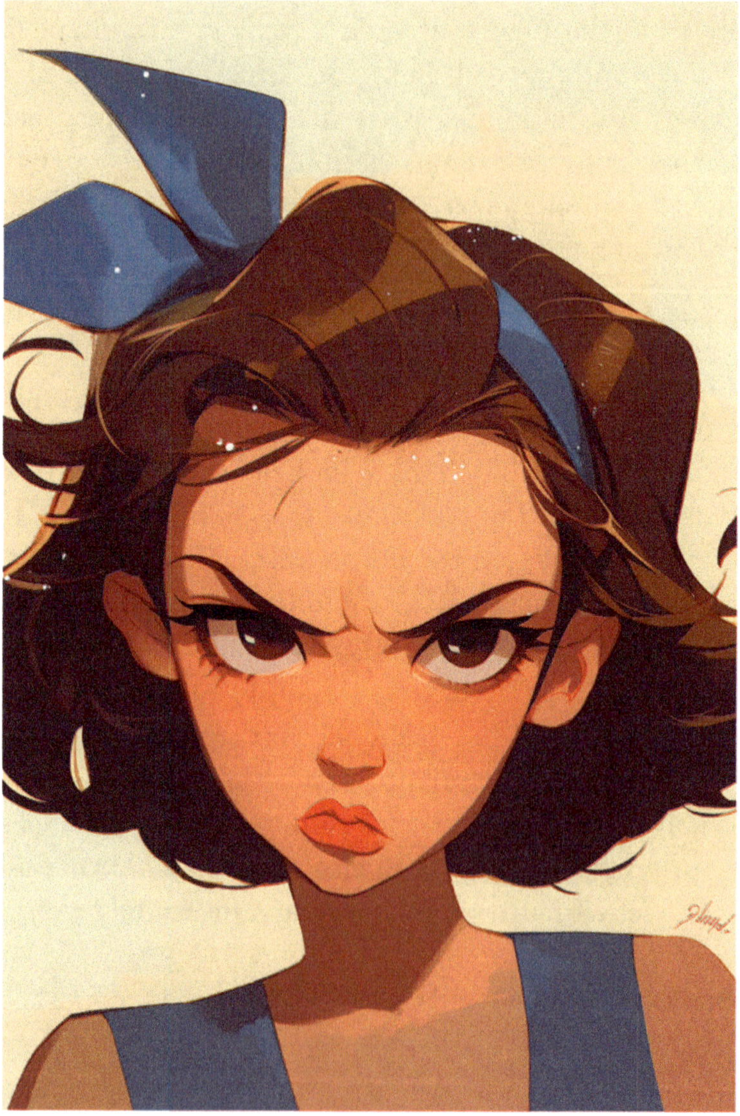

chapter 16

Professional setbacks and comebacks

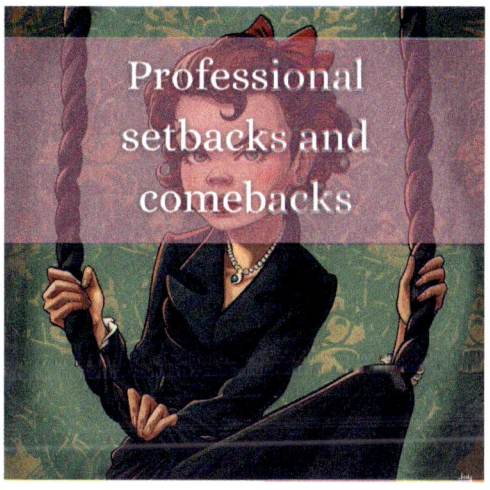

Judy Garland's career was not without its fair share of professional setbacks. Despite her immense talent and popularity, Garland faced numerous challenges that tested her resilience and showcased the dark side of Hollywood. From contract disputes to career slumps, she experienced moments when it seemed like her star was fading. However, true to her indomitable spirit, Garland always managed to stage spectacular comebacks that captivated audiences once again.

One of the major setbacks in Garland's career was her strained relationship with Metro-Goldwyn-Mayer (MGM), the studio that launched her to stardom. After her breakthrough in **The Wizard of Oz** (1939), MGM became both her lifeline and her captor. The studio recognized her exceptional talent and charisma, but as she grew older, they struggled to find roles that allowed her to evolve as an artist while still appealing to the mass audience. Garland longed to shed her wholesome, girl-next-door image and explore more complex characters, but the studio insisted on casting her in lightweight, predictable roles that perpetuated her **"girl next door"** persona.

The pressures placed on young starlets in Hollywood during that era left a lasting impact on Garland's mental and emotional well-being, often exacerbating her professional challenges. The studio's focus on her physical appearance, constant scrutiny, and rigorous demands took a toll on her self-esteem. Garland developed an unhealthy relationship with food and struggled with her weight throughout her career, leading to a cycle of insecurities that affected her performances and overall well-being.

Throughout the 1950s, Garland faced a series of box office failures that put a dent in her career. Despite her immense talent and dedication, she struggled to find roles that showcased her versatility and allowed her to break away from her established image. The studio's attempts to replicate her past success by casting her in similar roles led to a feeling of creative stagnation and audience fatigue. Garland yearned for projects that would challenge her and push the boundaries of her abilities, but the opportunities seemed elusive.

These setbacks were further compounded by personal issues, including her complicated relationships and battles with addiction, which affected her ability to consistently deliver on-screen. Garland's tumultuous love life, notably her marriages to David Rose, Vincente Minnelli, and Sid Luft, added emotional turmoil to her already demanding career. Her quest for stability and happiness often clashed with the chaotic and unpredictable nature of show business, leaving her vulnerable to the pitfalls of fame.

In 1954, Garland made a triumphant return to the stage in a historic concert at the London Palladium. This performance, known as the **"greatest night in show business history,"** showcased not only her extraordinary voice but also her genuine connection with the audience. Garland's vulnerability and sincerity on stage broke down the barriers, inviting the audience into her heart and soul. It was this emotional connection that reignited her career and proved that she still had the power to captivate audiences worldwide.

Garland's comeback continued with a string of successful films, including **A Star is Born** (1954), a role that showcased her acting range and solidified her status as one of Hollywood's most respected performers. In this raw and emotional portrayal, Garland masterfully depicted the rise and fall of a struggling artist, baring her own struggles and vulnerabilities to breathe life into the character. The film was both a critical and commercial success and earned her a well-deserved Academy Award nomination.

Throughout her comeback, Garland became renowned for her electrifying live performances. She embarked on successful concert tours, both nationally and internationally, where her magical stage presence and powerful voice stole the hearts of millions. Garland's live performances showcased her ability to express the deepest of emotions, from joy to heartbreak. Her songs became cathartic experiences for audiences, providing solace and hope during their own moments of struggle.

Her concerts were often sold-out events, drawing audiences from all walks of life. The diverse crowd that flocked to see Garland's performances reflected her universal appeal and the profound impact she had on people's lives. Garland's ability to connect emotionally with her audience transcended mere entertainment; it became a shared experience that touched the very core of human emotion. She became not just an entertainer but an empathetic friend, guiding her audience through their own joys and sorrows.

While Garland's career was marked by professional setbacks, it is her tenacity and resilience in the face of those challenges that set her apart. The hurdles Garland encountered throughout her journey only served to showcase her unwavering spirit and immense talent. Her ability to bounce back from career slumps and mesmerize audiences with her unparalleled vocal prowess remains an inspiration to this day. The legacy she left behind serves as a testament to the power of perseverance, reminding us that even in the face of adversity, true talent shines through, and legends are born.

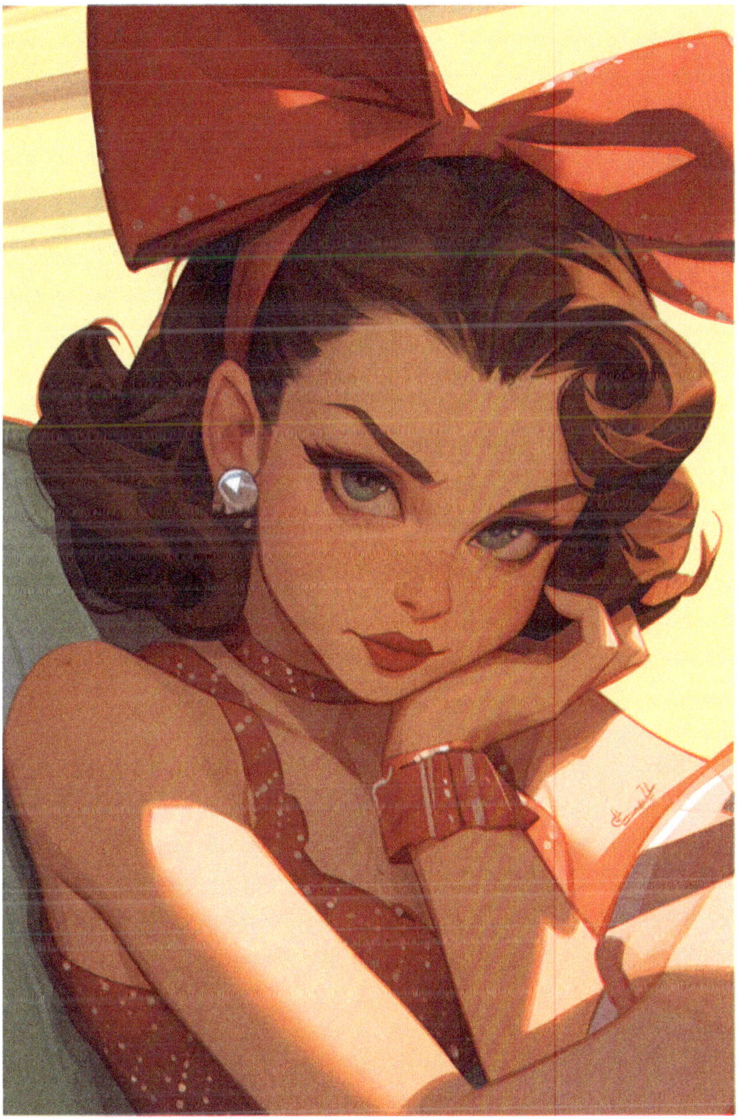

chapter 17

The relationship with fans and the media

Judy Garland's relationship with her fans was nothing short of extraordinary. It transcended the boundaries of a typical performer-audience dynamic, diving deep into the realm of genuine connection and mutual adoration. From the very beginning of her career, Garland captured the hearts and souls of her viewers with her rare talent and vulnerability, and in turn, they responded with a fervent dedication that would last a lifetime.

Throughout her career, Garland faced numerous personal struggles and professional setbacks, yet her fans stood by her side unwaveringly. They saw in her a reflection of their own joys and sorrows, finding solace and inspiration in her performances. Garland's gift for baring her soul on stage elicited an empathetic response from her fans, forging an unbreakable bond born of shared experiences and emotions.

Garland recognized the profound impact her fans had on her success and well-being, considering them an integral part of her journey. She understood that without their loyal support, she wouldn't have been able to navigate the tumultuous waters of the entertainment industry. In return, she made it a priority to connect with her fans, going above and beyond to show her appreciation and gratitude.

Her accessibility and genuine interactions set her apart from other celebrities of her time. Garland would often spend hours signing autographs, meeting fans at stage doors, and attending fan events. She reveled in these connections, cherishing the opportunity to personally thank her fans for their unwavering support and shower them with genuine warmth and affection.

But it was not just in the public eye that Garland valued her fans. Behind closed doors, she would dedicate time to personally respond to letters and gifts from her admirers. She kept countless scrapbooks filled with personal notes and mementos from fans, a testament to the deep connection she shared with them. This attention to detail and the investment of her time into her fans' lives was a true testament to her integrity and love for the people who had made her a star.

The bond between Garland and her fans was not confined to the realms of theatre and film alone. They became her extended family, often providing her with strength and motivation to carry on during moments of personal turmoil. Garland's fans were there to celebrate her triumphs, providing a resounding chorus of cheer and applause that echoed in her ears long after the curtain fell. Equally, they were there during her darkest moments, offering solace and reassurance that she was not alone.

To reciprocate the unwavering support she received, Garland also found solace in supporting causes close to her fans' hearts. She lent her voice to various charitable organizations, using her platform to raise awareness and funds for issues like child welfare and mental health. This further solidified the bond she shared with her fans, as they saw her not only as an entertainer but as a compassionate soul committed to making a difference in the world.

The media, too, played a significant role in shaping Garland's career and public image. From the early stages of her stardom, she found herself constantly under the watchful eye of the press. Her every move was dissected and analyzed, creating a constant whirlwind of attention and scrutiny.

While the media had the power to elevate or tarnish a celebrity's reputation, Garland managed to maintain a positive relationship with them. She recognized the importance of working in tandem with the press to promote her work and maintain public interest. Despite facing the occasional unfair criticism and invasive questioning, Garland handled herself with poise and grace, often using her quick wit and infectious personality to deflect negativity.

She understood that the media's portrayal of her had a direct impact on her relationship with her fans, and she consistently aimed to present herself in a manner that aligned with their genuine connection. Garland made a conscious effort to engage with interviewers and share glimpses of her true self, forging a deep sense of trust with her fans who felt like they truly knew her.

However, it would be remiss not to acknowledge the moments when Garland clashed with the media. As a strong-willed individual and an advocate for artists' rights, she was unafraid to use her platform to speak out against the paradoxical nature of the industry. She vocalized her frustrations with the pressures and exploitations she encountered, both endorsing and embodying the struggles faced by countless artists.

These instances of transparency and honesty endeared Garland even further to her fans, who saw in her a fearless champion fighting not only for herself but for their collective struggles. Her willingness to stand up against the powers that be, demanding fair treatment and sincere portrayal, only further cemented her status as an icon who transcended the boundaries of her profession.

Through the ups and downs, Garland's relationship with her fans and the media remained an ever-present and vital aspect of her life. She relied on the unwavering support and adoration of her fans to lift her up during challenging times, and she often sought solace in the profound connection she shared with them. In turn, her fans reciprocated, continuing to champion her work and shower her with love and support.

Even after her untimely passing, Garland's legacy and the bond she shared with her fans endure. Her music, films, and performances continue to resonate with audiences across generations, attracting new admirers who appreciate her emotive and captivating artistry. The relationship between Judy Garland, her fans, and the media serves as a timeless testament to the power of genuine talent, authenticity, and the enduring impact that one person can have on the world.

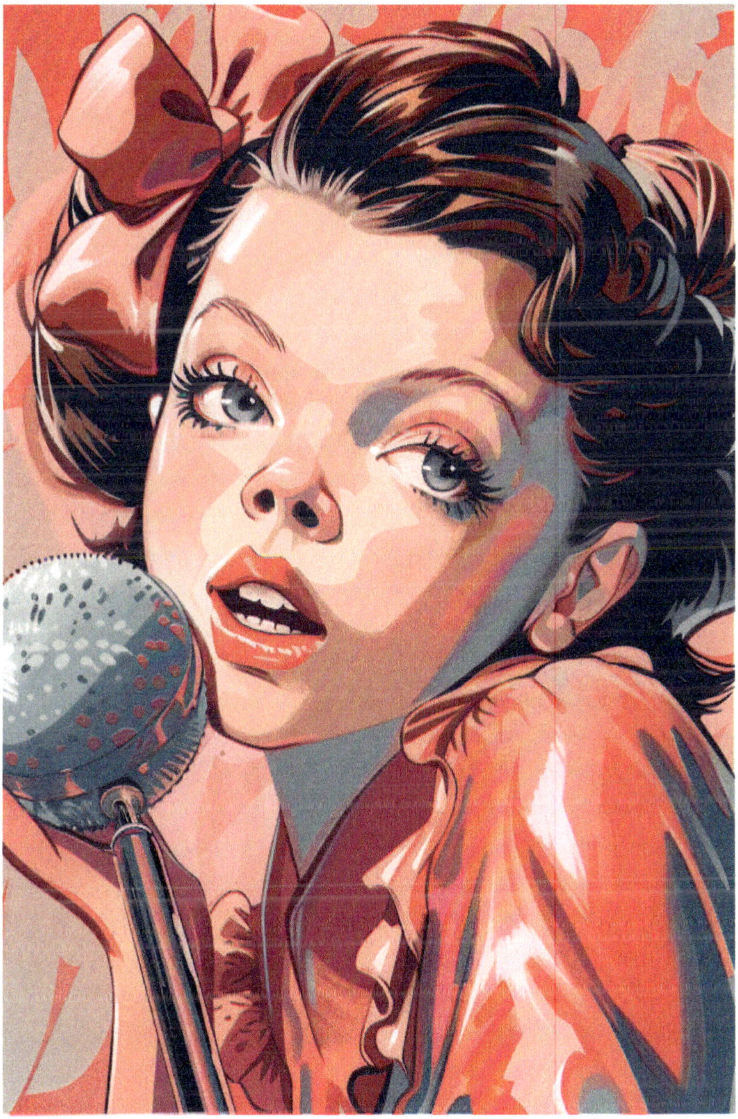

THE LATER YEARS

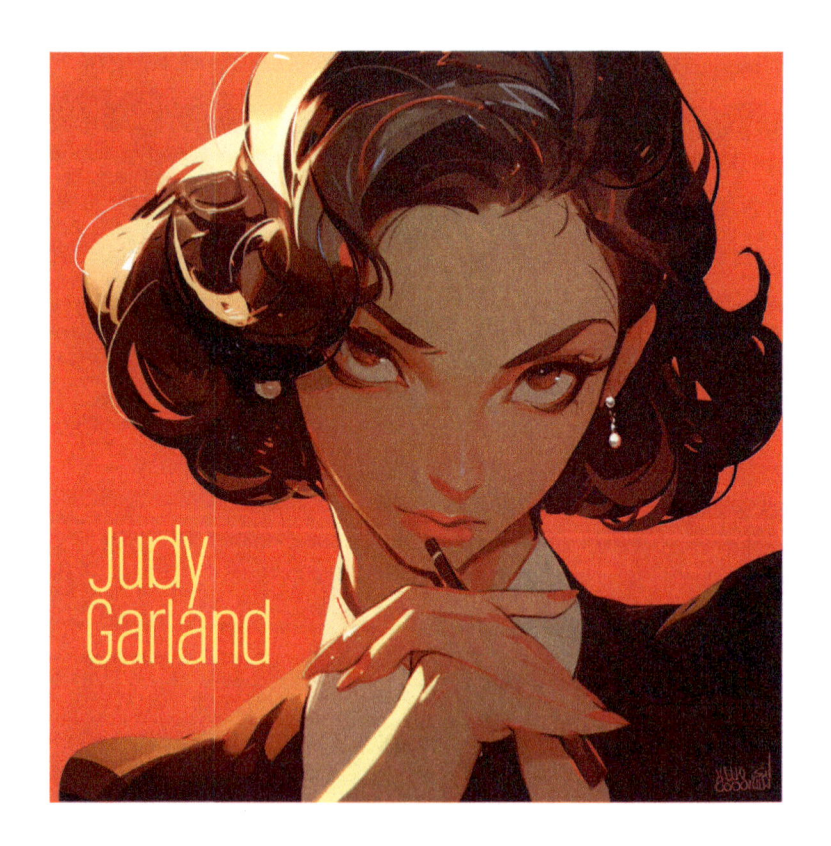

chapter 18

Transition to television and live performances

Throughout her illustrious career, Judy Garland captivated audiences both on the silver screen and the stage. As the years went by, Garland found new avenues to showcase her exceptional talent, transitioning from movies to television and live performances. This chapter delves into this transformative period of Garland's career and explores the impact she made in these mediums.

In the 1950s, Garland's career saw a shift as she began to venture into the realm of television. This move allowed her to reach a broader audience and solidify her status as one of the greatest entertainers of her time. Television, with its intimate nature, provided Garland an opportunity to connect with viewers on a personal level. She made numerous appearances on popular variety shows, such as "The Ed Sullivan Show," "The Jack Paar Tonight Show," and "The Dinah Shore Show," captivating audiences with her infectious energy and unparalleled stage presence.

During her television performances, Garland showcased her prodigious singing prowess and acting abilities. Whether she was belting out a show-stopping number or bringing tears to the eyes of viewers with a heartfelt ballad, Garland had the remarkable ability to make viewers feel every emotion she conveyed. Her tone, phrasing, and effortless vocal control brought to life the lyrics and melodies, leaving the audience captivated and deeply moved.

Garland's presence on television was not limited to musical performances alone. She also showcased her comedic talents and irresistible charm through guest appearances on popular sitcoms and variety shows. Her natural comedic timing and infectious laughter delighted viewers, further solidifying her status as a multi-talented entertainer.

In addition to her success on television, Garland embarked on exhilarating live performances that left an indelible mark on all those fortunate enough to witness them. She took her extraordinary talent to concert halls across the United States and Europe, captivating audiences with her powerful voice, emotional delivery, and magnetic stage presence.

One notable chapter in Garland's transition to live performances was her historic run at the Palace Theatre in New York City in 1951. This engagement lasted for an unprecedented 19 weeks, breaking box office records and solidifying her as a star of immense magnitude. Garland's residency at the Palace Theatre became a cultural phenomenon, with fans flocking from near and far to witness her electrifying performances. Every night, the theater was filled with anticipation and excitement as Garland graced the stage and effortlessly took the audience on a journey through her music.

Garland's live performances were more than just concerts; they were transformative experiences that bridged the gap between artist and audience. With each song, she bared her soul, allowing audiences to feel her joys, sorrows, hopes, and vulnerabilities. Her performances were filled with moments of vulnerability and authenticity, as she openly shared her personal struggles and triumphs with her fans. This genuine connection created an unparalleled bond, turning each performance into a collective experience of shared emotions.

The impact of Garland's live performances extended far beyond the concert hall. Her ability to connect with audiences on such a profound level inspired countless individuals and left an indelible mark on the world of entertainment. Many artists who followed in her footsteps cited Garland as a source of inspiration, not just for her talent, but for her ability to connect with audiences on an emotional level.

In conclusion, chapter 18 delves into Judy Garland's transition from movies to television and live performances, showcasing the impact she made in these mediums. Her television appearances allowed her to connect with viewers in an intimate setting, while her live performances created transformative experiences for audiences. Garland's talent, versatility, and ability to forge deep connections with viewers and audiences further solidified her status as a beloved and iconic entertainer.

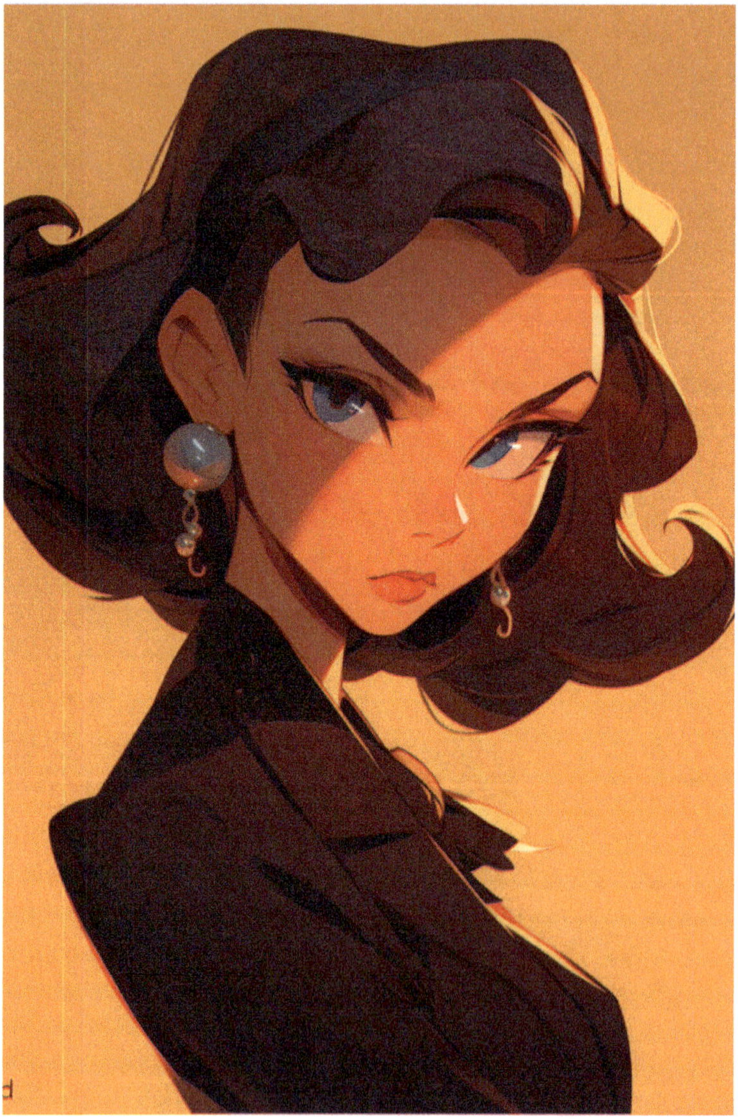

chapter 19

Notable works and achievements in the latter part of her career

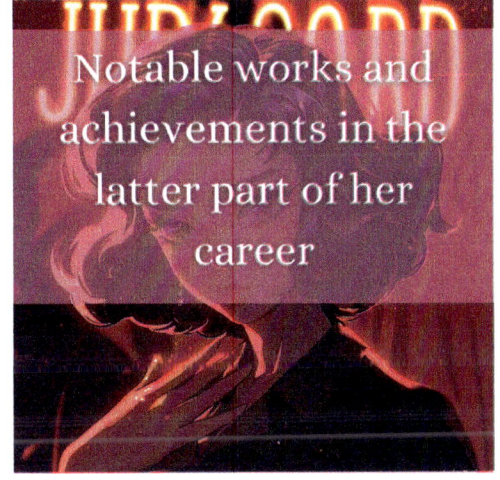

Judy Garland's career spanned several decades, and even after her breakout role in "The Wizard of Oz," she continued to deliver remarkable performances and leave a lasting impact on the entertainment industry. In the latter part of her career, Garland's work showcased her versatility as an actress and performer, solidifying her as a true legend in the annals of show business.

One of Garland's notable works during this period is her role in the 1954 film "A Star Is Born." Directed by George Cukor, this musical drama portrayed the rise of a young actress, Esther Blodgett, played by Garland, whose talent and dreams ultimately clash with the self-destructive journey of her husband, Norman Maine, portrayed by James Mason. Garland's performance in this film was hailed by critics and audiences alike as one of her finest. Her ability to bring vulnerability, passion, and raw emotion to her character's journey earned her a nomination for the Academy Award for Best Actress, a testament to her exceptional talent. While she didn't win the Oscar that year, her performance in "A Star Is Born" has become an enduring part of cinematic history and is often cited as one of the best of her career.

Another noteworthy achievement in Garland's later career was her successful transition to television. In the 1960s, she hosted her own television series, "The Judy Garland Show." This variety show provided a platform for Garland to showcase her incredible singing ability, dance skills, and charismatic stage presence. Each episode featured guest stars, musical performances, and comedic sketches, all of which highlighted the multi-faceted talent of the beloved entertainer. Despite the high production costs and stiff competition from other shows at the time, "The Judy Garland Show" further solidified Garland's status as a cultural icon. Although the show was sadly canceled after only one season due to financial pressures and Garland's struggles with personal issues, it remains a testament to her enduring appeal and talent, as well as her desire to bring joy and entertainment to her fans through different mediums.

During this period, Garland also continued to dazzle audiences with her live performances. Her concerts were legendary displays of her talent, as she captivated audiences with her emotive voice and mesmerizing stage presence. The pinnacle of her live performances came in April 1961 when she delivered an unforgettable concert at Carnegie Hall in New York City. This landmark event, often referred to as the "greatest night in show business history," showcased Garland at the height of her artistic prowess. Her stirring renditions of beloved songs like "Over the Rainbow," "The Man That Got Away," and "By Myself" left audiences spellbound, earning her a standing ovation and widespread critical acclaim. The live album capturing this iconic performance went on to win four Grammy Awards, including Album of the Year, Best Female Vocal Performance, and Best Engineering Contribution. It also remained on the Billboard album charts for 73 weeks, solidifying its place as one of the best-selling live albums of all time. Garland's live performances not only displayed her extraordinary talent but also showcased her ability to connect with her audience on a profound level, making each performance an unforgettable experience for those lucky enough to witness them.

Additionally, Garland ventured into the realm of recording, releasing several successful albums in her later career. These albums not only showcased her vocal range and emotional depth but also demonstrated her versatility in interpreting a wide range of musical styles. From jazz standards to Broadway show tunes, Garland's recordings captivated listeners and further showcased her remarkable ability to breathe new life into beloved songs. With each album, she continued to evolve as an artist, experimenting with different arrangements and exploring new musical territories.

In acknowledgment of her extraordinary contributions to the entertainment industry, Garland received numerous accolades later in her career. In 1997, she was awarded a posthumous Grammy Lifetime Achievement Award, recognizing her indelible mark on the music industry and her lasting influence. Furthermore, her iconic recording of "Over the Rainbow" was inducted into the Grammy Hall of Fame, honoring its timeless impact and enduring popularity. Additionally, Garland was honored with a star on the Hollywood Walk of Fame, solidifying her status as a true Hollywood icon whose legacy would forever be etched in the hearts of millions.

Through her notable works and achievements in the latter part of her career, Judy Garland continued to solidify her legacy as one of the greatest entertainers of all time. Her performances on screen, television, and stage, as well as her contributions to the music industry, left an indelible mark on popular culture that continues to inspire and captivate audiences to this day. Garland's enduring talent and ability to connect with audiences on a deep emotional level truly make her a timeless legend in the world of entertainment.

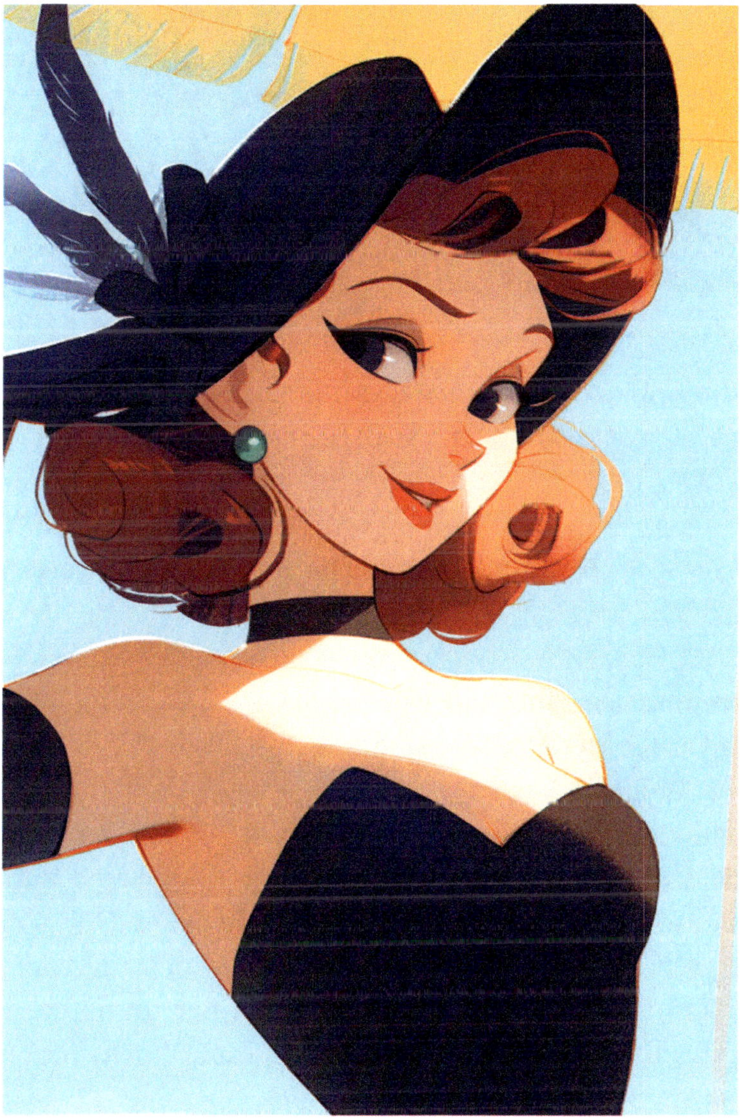

chapter 20

Reflections on her legacy by contemporaries and Garland herself

Judy Garland, a name that continues to resonate throughout the ages as a beacon of talent and resilience. In this chapter, we delve deep into the reflections and perspectives on Garland's legacy from both her contemporaries and the woman herself, exploring the profound impact she had on the entertainment industry and society as a whole.

Contemporaries who had the privilege of working with Judy Garland offer invaluable insights into the depth of her talent and the indomitable spirit she possessed. Co-stars, directors, and fellow performers recall with awe the way Garland effortlessly commanded the stage, leaving audiences spellbound with her passionate performances. Her ability to evoke genuine emotion in her renditions of songs and bring characters to life was unparalleled, with her unmatched voice sending shivers down the spines of those lucky enough to witness it.

One of the individuals profoundly affected by Garland's talent was Mickey Rooney, her co-star in numerous films throughout their careers. Rooney reminisced about their time together, stating, "Judy Garland had a gift that was inexplicable. She possessed an innate ability to reach the depths of emotion that few could dare to touch. Working with her was both a joy and a challenge, as she continuously pushed the boundaries of her craft. There was a rawness and vulnerability about her performances that left a lasting impact on all who were fortunate enough to witness it."

Vincente Minnelli, who directed Garland in multiple iconic films including "Meet Me in St. Louis" and "The Clock," also shared his thoughts on her talent and work ethic. He expressed, "Judy was a force of nature. She had an unmatched work ethic and a determination to give the best performance possible. It was inspiring to witness her passion for her craft and her unwavering commitment to her audience. She had this extraordinary ability to infuse every role with a piece of her own soul, creating characters that were both relatable and timeless."

Beyond her co-stars and directors, the impact of Garland's talent was felt by fans around the world. Her unique ability to empathize with audiences of all ages and backgrounds created an intimate connection that transcended the barriers of time and space. Her performances were more than just entertainment; they were a balm for the soul, a connection to the depths of human emotion that few artists could channel so effortlessly.

Garland's legacy extended far beyond her on-screen presence. Her music, with its timeless lyrics and haunting melodies, continues to captivate listeners, transporting them to an era when Hollywood was at its zenith. From her iconic rendition of "Over the Rainbow" in "The Wizard of Oz" to her heartfelt ballads in "A Star is Born," Garland's voice remains a testament to the power of music to touch the deepest corners of the human heart.

Yet, beneath the shining façade of her performances, Garland faced a lifetime of struggles and personal demons. She openly discussed her battles with addiction, the pressures of fame, and the constant need to maintain a certain image. Her honesty and vulnerability in speaking about these challenges endeared her to millions, and her ability to find strength in her darkest moments became a beacon of hope for those facing their own hardships.

In her own words, Garland reflected on her career with a mix of pride and introspection. She acknowledged the weight of the expectations placed upon her from an early age, as she became an overnight sensation in Hollywood. "I was thrust into the spotlight at such a young age. There were moments when the pressure felt unbearable, and I struggled to prove myself over and over again. But what kept me going was my love for performing, for connecting with audiences. That's what I lived for, and that's what pushed me to keep going despite the challenges."

Garland's love for connecting with audiences, feeling their energy fuel her performances, and the pure bliss of being on stage demonstrated her unyielding passion for her art. She recognized the power that her voice and presence held, and it was this realization that allowed her to leave an indelible mark on generations to come.

One of the most significant aspects of Judy Garland's legacy is its resounding impact on LGBTQ+ communities. Her struggles and resilience struck a chord with a marginalized group yearning for acceptance and understanding. Garland emerged as an icon, encapsulating the spirit of the LGBTQ+ community, and her performances became showcases of self-expression, love, and acceptance. From Stonewall to today's Pride parades, her songs and performances ignite a sense of belonging, unity, and the undeniable power of being true to oneself.

This chapter also delves into the various tribute performances and memorials that have served to keep Judy Garland's legacy alive. Broadway revivals, concerts, and commemorative events pay homage to her immense talent and the timeless impact she had on the world. Through these tributes, a new generation of artists can experience the magic she brought to the stage and connect with the raw emotions she channeled so flawlessly.

In conclusion, the reflections on Judy Garland's legacy by both her contemporaries and the woman herself reveal the profound and lasting impact she had on the entertainment industry and society at large. Her unparalleled talent, dedication, and vulnerability continue to inspire actors, musicians, and fans alike. Judy Garland's legacy stands as a testament to the power of artistic expression and the ability of one person's genuine authenticity to touch the hearts and leave an everlasting imprint on the world.

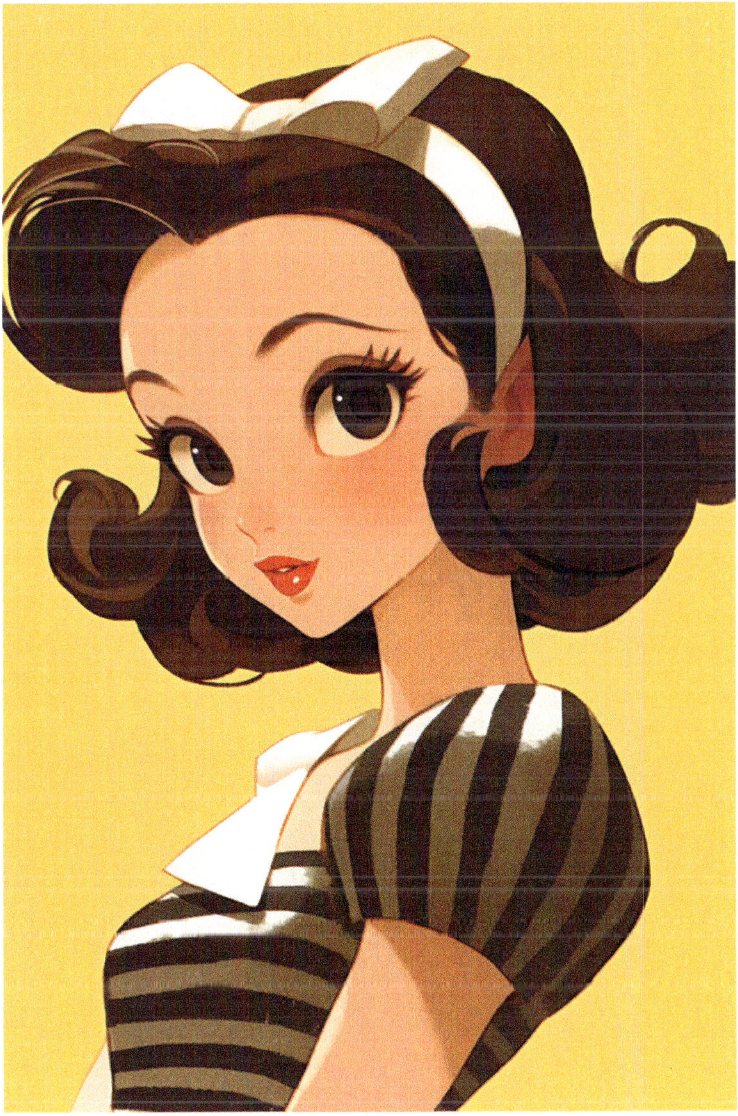

THE ICON OFF-SCREEN

chapter 21

Judy Garland as a mother and friend

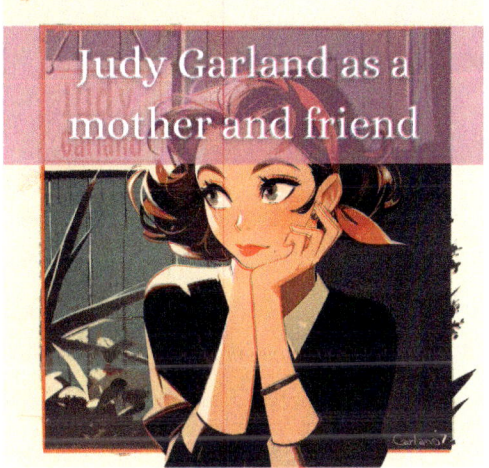

Throughout her life, Judy Garland not only captivated audiences with her exceptional talent, but she also held the cherished roles of mother and friend. Behind the glittering lights of Hollywood, Garland's personal life was shaped by her deep connections with her children and her close circle of friends.

As a mother, Judy Garland faced numerous challenges, but her unwavering love for her children was evident in every aspect of her life. She had three children: Liza Minnelli, Lorna Luft, and Joey Luft. Garland's relationship with her children was characterized by a unique blend of joy, struggle, and sacrifice. From an early age, she instilled in them a love for the arts and supported their endeavors in show business.

Liza Minnelli, Garland's eldest daughter, not only inherited her mother's talent but also her incredible resilience. With the same determination and spirit that made Garland a star, Minnelli forged her own successful career as a singer and actress. Their bond was complex, as they shared both an unbreakable love and an understanding of the immense pressure that came with being part of the Garland legacy.

Minnelli witnessed firsthand the highs and lows of her mother's life, from Garland's rise to stardom in "The Wizard of Oz" to her battle with addiction and personal struggles. Yet, despite the challenges, they navigated the ups and downs together, relying on each other for support and understanding. Garland's love for Minnelli was unwavering, and she often drew strength from her daughter's accomplishments, finding solace in the fact that she had passed on her own indomitable spirit and determination.

Lorna Luft, the middle child, also pursued a career in show business, tirelessly striving to carve her own path. Garland's relationship with Lorna was marked by a special tenderness, as Lorna often sought solace in her mother's embrace. Despite Garland's own struggles with addiction and personal demons, she fought fiercely to shield her children from the harshness of the world they were born into.

Garland recognized the immense talent in Lorna and encouraged her to develop her artistic abilities. Lorna would often join her mother on stage, gaining valuable experience and honing her skills. Through the years, Garland's unconditional love for her daughter was a constant source of strength for both of them, providing a safe haven amidst the chaotic nature of the entertainment industry.

Joey Luft, Garland's only son, chose a different path in life, away from the spotlight that had surrounded his mother and sisters. Garland deeply valued Joey's decision and respected his desire for a more private existence. Despite the physical separation, their bond remained unbreakable, as Garland's love for her son transcended stardom.

Garland cherished the moments she spent with Joey, treasuring their private conversations and the simple joys of being a mother. She filled his life with love, support, and guidance, although she faced her own struggles and battles. Joey found solace in his mother's unconditional love, finding comfort in knowing that he was cherished and accepted just as he was.

In addition to her role as a mother, Judy Garland cherished her friendships with fellow actors and musicians. These deep connections allowed her to find solace and understanding in an industry that often chewed up and spit out its stars. One of her most influential and enduring friendships was with Mickey Rooney.

Their friendship began when they were both young stars at MGM, and it only grew stronger as they navigated the challenges of the entertainment industry together. Rooney became not only a close confidant but also a tireless advocate for Garland, always believing in her talent and supporting her through both triumphs and tribulations. Through their shared experiences, they built a bond that went beyond the screen, forged by mutual admiration and a deep understanding of the unique pressures they faced as child stars.

Garland also found solace in the company of legends such as Frank Sinatra and Tony Bennett. These friendships extended beyond mere acquaintanceship, as they became her pillars of support during times of uncertainty and personal struggles. Sinatra, who had faced his own demons, understood Garland's struggles intimately, and their connection ran deep.

Tony Bennett, with whom Garland shared a love for music, provided her with unwavering support and a sense of camaraderie. They celebrated each other's successes, championing the greatness they saw in each other's performances. These genuine and lasting friendships provided Garland with an invaluable support system that she often sought refuge in throughout her career.

However, Garland's personal struggles and the pressures of her career sometimes strained her relationships, causing rifts with her closest friends. The toll of her health issues, combined with the demands of the entertainment industry, could weigh heavily on her emotional well-being. She battled with addiction and relied on medication to cope with the challenges she faced.

Yet, true friends stood by her side, understanding the complexities of her journey and offering unwavering support. They recognized that the woman behind the iconic voice and captivating performances was a fragile soul who needed compassion and understanding. They remained steadfast, even when Garland's struggles threatened to overpower her.

Ultimately, Judy Garland's legacy as a mother and friend is a testament to her remarkable capacity to love, nurture, and care for those closest to her. Her devotion to her children and the intimate connections she formed with her friends reveal a side of Garland that went beyond the stage. As much as she influenced the entertainment industry with her talent, she also made a profound impact on the hearts and lives of those she loved and cherished.

Garland's journey as a mother and friend was not always easy, but she faced each challenge with her characteristic resilience and determination. Her ability to navigate the complexities of fame while maintaining meaningful relationships serves as a poignant reminder of her humanity, strength, and enduring spirit. Even in the face of her own struggles, she left an indelible impression on those fortunate enough to call her mother and friend, touching their lives with love, inspiration, and the magic that was uniquely Judy Garland.

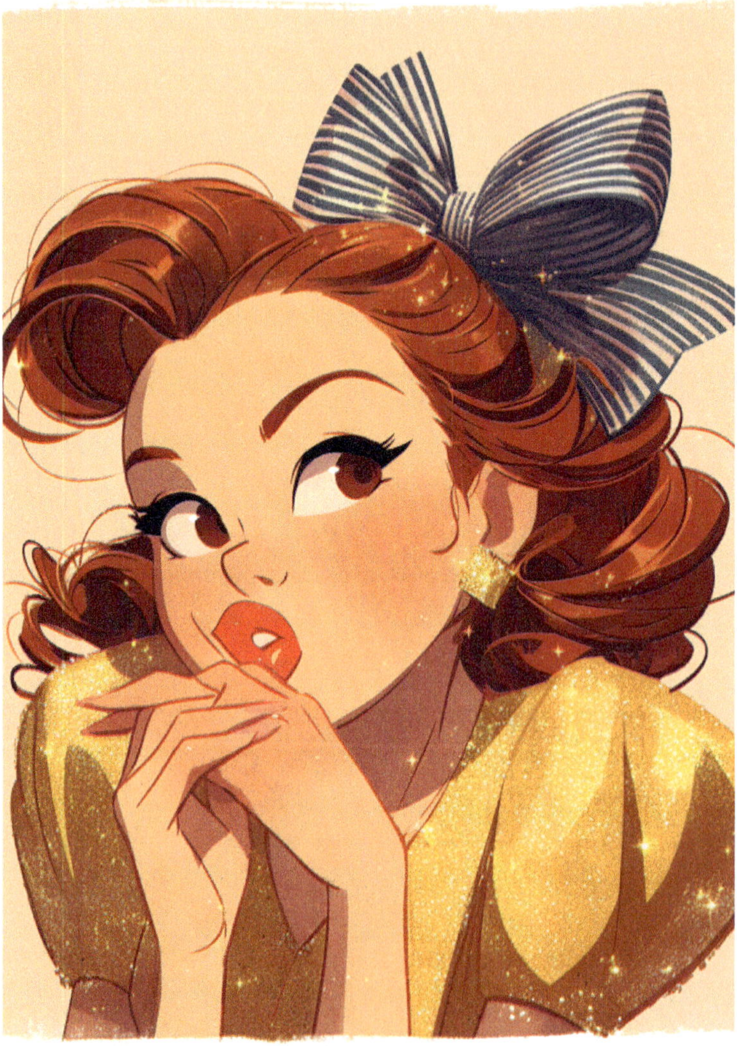

chapter 22

Philanthropy and personal interests

Judy Garland's philanthropic endeavors and personal interests were an integral part of her life and reflected her genuine compassion for others. Throughout her career, she worked tirelessly to use her fame and influence for charitable causes, leaving a lasting impact on those in need.

One of Garland's remarkable philanthropic efforts was her involvement with the American Cancer Society. Having experienced health struggles herself, she understood the physical and emotional toll that cancer takes on individuals and their families. As a result, she dedicated her time and energy to raise awareness and funds for cancer research, frequently participating in benefit concerts and events. Her performances often became opportunities to highlight the urgent need for continued research, improved treatment options, and support services for patients. Garland's heartfelt dedication to this cause inspired many and helped shed light on the importance of funding cancer research.

In addition to her work with the American Cancer Society, Garland championed numerous other charitable endeavors. She was deeply passionate about children's welfare, especially for those facing hardships. Garland not only financially supported organizations dedicated to children's causes, but she also actively participated and engaged in their initiatives. Among her many contributions, Garland became a founding member of the Clara Barton Open Air School, a groundbreaking institution that catered to children with disabilities. This hands-on involvement allowed her to directly impact the lives of these young individuals, offering companionship, encouragement, and support. By leveraging her platform and resources, Garland brought attention to the importance of inclusion and equal opportunities for all children, regardless of their abilities or circumstances.

Beyond her dedication to child welfare, Garland was deeply committed to advocating for animal rights. Her love for animals was evident in her personal life, as she owned a variety of pets and spoke out against animal cruelty. Garland believed in using her influence to raise awareness about the unjust treatment of animals in various industries. She publicly condemned practices such as animal testing, fur farming, and circuses that exploited animals for entertainment purposes. She actively supported animal rescue organizations, making personal donations to facilities that provided care and shelter for animals in need. Garland's passion for protecting all creatures, big and small, was evident in her actions, setting an example for others to follow in their own advocacy efforts.

In addition to her philanthropy, Garland had a profound appreciation for the arts and literature. As an artist, she understood the power of storytelling, both on and off the screen. Garland surrounded herself with books and was an avid reader across various genres. She found inspiration in the works of renowned authors, connecting with their thoughts and ideas. Her personal collection of books was extensive, showcasing her wide range of interests and intellectual curiosity. Whether through poetry, fiction, or non-fiction, Garland found solace and artistic stimulation within the pages of these treasured volumes. She often turned to literature to find comfort, escape, and personal growth, demonstrating the profound impact that books can have in shaping one's worldview.

Aside from her love for literature, Garland also found solace and joy in tending to her garden. Gardening provided her with a sanctuary within her own home, allowing her to recharge her spirit amidst the chaos of the entertainment industry. She spent hours cultivating and nurturing various plants and flowers, using her green thumb to create a vibrant and peaceful environment. Garland's love for gardening extended beyond aesthetics; she saw it as a way to connect with nature and find balance in her life. Through her garden, she found a sense of peace and contentment, reaffirming her deep appreciation for the natural world and its ability to heal and inspire.

Overall, Judy Garland's philanthropy and personal interests reveal a multi-dimensional individual who not only captivated audiences with her performances but also demonstrated a genuine desire to make a positive impact on society. Her commitment to various causes, such as cancer research, child welfare, animal rights, and her passion for literature and gardening, showcase the depth of her character beyond the glamorous facade of Hollywood. Garland's enduring legacy extends far beyond her talent as an entertainer, leaving behind a legacy of compassion, inspiration, and a true commitment to improving the lives of others by leveraging her platform for positive change in the world.

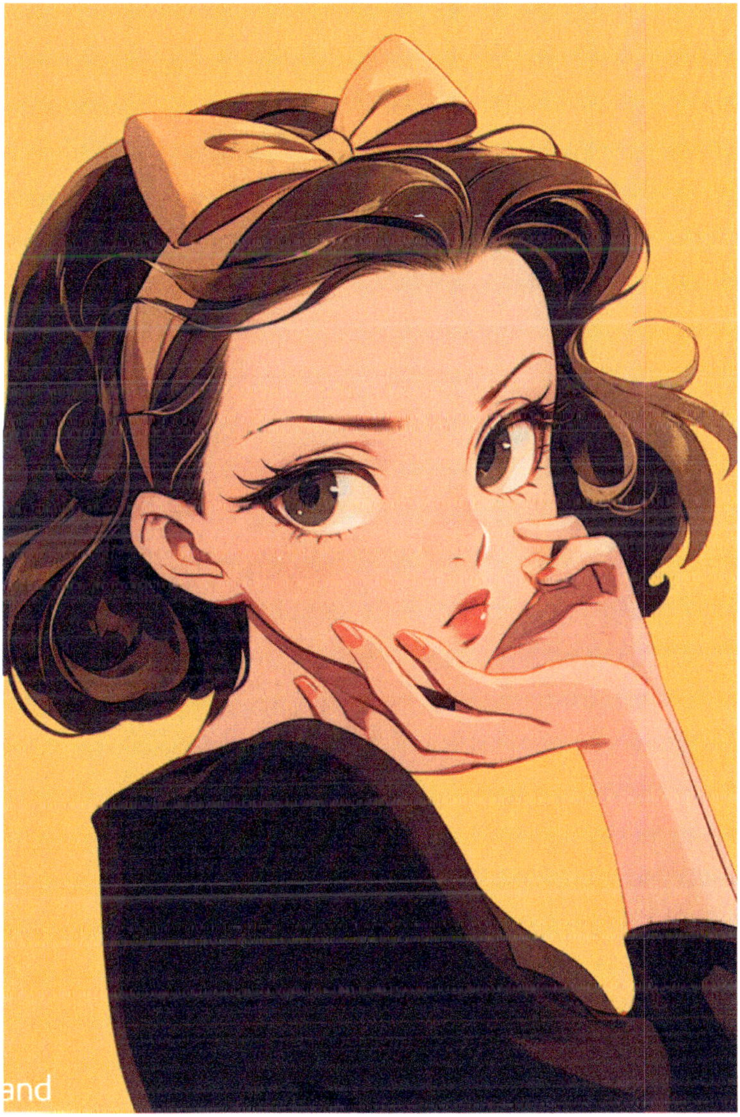
and

chapter 23

Garland's influence on fashion and public image

Judy Garland's impact on fashion and her public image was undeniable. From the moment she burst onto the screen as Dorothy in **The Wizard of Oz**, Garland became a fashion icon, known for her youthful and charming style. Her signature blue gingham dress, paired with ruby slippers, has become an enduring symbol of innocence and adventure. This iconic outfit, designed by legendary costumer Adrian, has left an indelible mark on popular culture and has been replicated and referenced in various forms of media for decades.

As Garland ventured further into her career, her influence expanded beyond her role in **The Wizard of Oz**. Through her timeless performances in films such as **Meet Me in St. Louis** and **A Star is Born**, Garland captured the hearts of audiences across the world, and her fashion choices began to reflect her evolving persona. Embracing maturity, Garland's style transformed, showcasing a newfound sophistication and elegance.

One of the key elements of Garland's style was her emphasis on natural beauty. Unlike many of her contemporaries in the Hollywood spotlight, Garland preferred minimal makeup and often wore her hair in simple, natural styles. This understated approach to beauty resonated with her fans, who admired her for her relatability and genuine persona. Garland's emphasis on natural beauty became a trendsetter at the time, aligning with the evolving societal shift towards embracing individuality and authenticity.

Garland also embraced the power of accessories to enhance her personal style. From oversized hats to statement jewelry, she used these pieces to add intrigue and color to her outfits. Her collection of hats, in particular, became highly sought after, with fans clamoring to own a piece of Garland's iconic fashion. The unmistakable charm of her accessories helped solidify her status as a fashion maverick, inspiring countless individuals to experiment with their own fashion choices.

Another aspect of Judy Garland's influence on fashion was her ability to dress with confidence and express her own unique sense of style. She fearlessly experimented with different looks, incorporating bold colors, daring silhouettes, and unconventional accessories. Garland's playful audacity and unwavering self-assurance solidified her status as a fashion trailblazer, inspiring countless individuals to embrace their own personal style and take risks with their fashion choices.

Garland's public image played a significant role in shaping her fashion impact. She was admired for her down-to-earth personality and relatable charm, making her an inspiration to women of all ages. Her resilience in the face of personal struggles endeared her to the public, and her ability to connect with audiences through her performances made her a beloved figure worldwide. This admiration for Garland as a person translated into an interest in her fashion choices, with fans aspiring to recreate her looks and capture a piece of her timeless style.

Furthermore, Garland's influence extended beyond the glamorous world of Hollywood. Recognizing her status as a cultural icon, renowned fashion houses drew inspiration from her classic, refined look. Designers sought to capture the elegance and grace exhibited by Garland through their collections, paying homage to her enduring legacy. Some even collaborated with her directly, such as her work as a spokeswoman for the fashion label "Miss Ireland Galway," which capitalized on her wholesome, girl-next-door image to sell their garments. Her distinct style continues to be referenced and emulated, reinforcing Garland's status as an influential figure in the fashion industry.

In understanding Garland's impact on fashion, one must acknowledge her ability to transcend trends and remain relevant throughout the years. Her fashion choices remain timeless, speaking to the enduring allure of her style. Garland effortlessly embodied both glamour and casual elegance, showcasing her versatility and adaptability to different roles on and off-screen.

Through her fashion and public image, Judy Garland left an indelible mark on popular culture. Her natural beauty, timeless elegance, and ability to exude confidence continue to inspire designers, fashion enthusiasts, and fans alike. Even decades after her passing, Garland's fashion legacy serves as a testament to her enduring appeal and stands as a reminder of the profound impact she made during her career.

chatvariety.com

THE LEGACY LIVES ON

chapter 24

Garland's impact on future generations of actors and musicians

Judy Garland, a name that resonates with a timeless appeal, had a profound and enduring impact on future generations of actors and musicians. Her incredible talent, undeniable charisma, and indomitable spirit have left an indelible mark on the world of entertainment. Let us delve even deeper into the essence of Garland's transformative influence, exploring the depths of her artistry and the lasting legacy she has bestowed upon the performing arts.

One of the key facets of Garland's influence lies in her innate ability to connect with audiences on an emotional level. Her performances were not mere acts; they were powerful journeys that evoked a wide range of emotions in the hearts of those who witnessed them. Garland possessed the rare gift of translating intangible human emotions into tangible forms, touching the depths of the soul. Her evocative vocal renditions of timeless classics such as "Over the Rainbow" and "The Man That Got Away" still resonate with listeners today, as her voice seamlessly weaved together passion, vulnerability, and raw power. These timeless melodies became a conduit for emotional release, allowing audiences to explore the depths of their own feelings through Garland's mesmerizing performances. The impact of her emotional authenticity continues to reverberate in the works of contemporary actors and musicians who aspire to create connections that transcend the boundaries between performer and audience.

In addition to her remarkable ability to evoke emotions, Garland's influence also lies in her exceptional talent as both an actress and a singer. She seamlessly transitioned between creating memorable characters and delivering captivating musical performances, blurring the lines between film and music. Garland was a true performer in every sense, combining her acting prowess with her vocal skills to create truly transformative works of art. Her characters were not mere figments of imagination; they were vessels through which she channeled her own experiences, struggles, and triumphs. Whether she was portraying the hopeful and ambitious Esther Blodgett in "A Star Is Born" or the tormented and tenacious Vicki Lester in "The Wizard of Oz," Garland imbued each role with a depth and authenticity that resonated with audiences on a profound level. Her ability to seamlessly blend acting and singing served as a beacon of inspiration for future artists who recognized the potential of combining various art forms to create a singular, captivating experience for audiences.

Beyond her artistic legacy, Garland's impact extended to her role as a trailblazer in the entertainment industry. She emerged during a time when the studio system exerted tight control over actors and their creative endeavors. Garland's courageous rebellion against the oppressive studio system and her vocal advocacy for fair treatment and creative autonomy inspired future generations to fight for their rights as artists. She took a stand against the exploitative practices that were pervasive during that era, paving the way for a more equitable and inclusive industry. Garland's struggles and triumphs became an emblem of resilience and empowerment, encouraging artists to assert their creative voices and challenge the established norms of the industry. Her fearless pursuit of independence continues to serve as a reminder for artists today to never compromise their artistic integrity and to fight for the recognition and fair treatment that every artist deserves.

Moreover, Garland's enduring influence can be observed in the thematic depth and introspection that permeates the works of countless artists today. She fearlessly embraced and conveyed complex emotions, tackling challenging subjects and exploring the human condition with unflinching authenticity. By navigating the depths of her own emotions, Garland showed future performers the transformative power of vulnerability and the ability to evoke empathy. Her willingness to confront the darkest corners of the human psyche opened doors for subsequent artists to explore a wider range of themes and narratives. Inspired by her courage, artists today continue to push boundaries, challenge societal norms, and share their personal stories with unapologetic honesty. The influence of Garland's candor can be witnessed in the transformative power of contemporary art that dares to delve into the complexities of the human experience, inviting audiences to reflect, grow, and connect on a profoundly deeper level.

In conclusion, Judy Garland's impact on future generations of actors and musicians reverberates through the annals of entertainment history. Her ability to forge emotional connections, seamlessly blend acting and singing, challenge industry norms, and explore complex themes with unflinching authenticity has forever shaped the landscape of the performing arts. Garland's artistic legacy continues to inspire present-day artists to strive for emotional authenticity, artistic versatility, and social change. Through her enduring influence, Judy Garland illuminates the path for performers who seek to forge their own unique mark on the world, leaving an everlasting legacy as an artist and an icon of the human spirit.

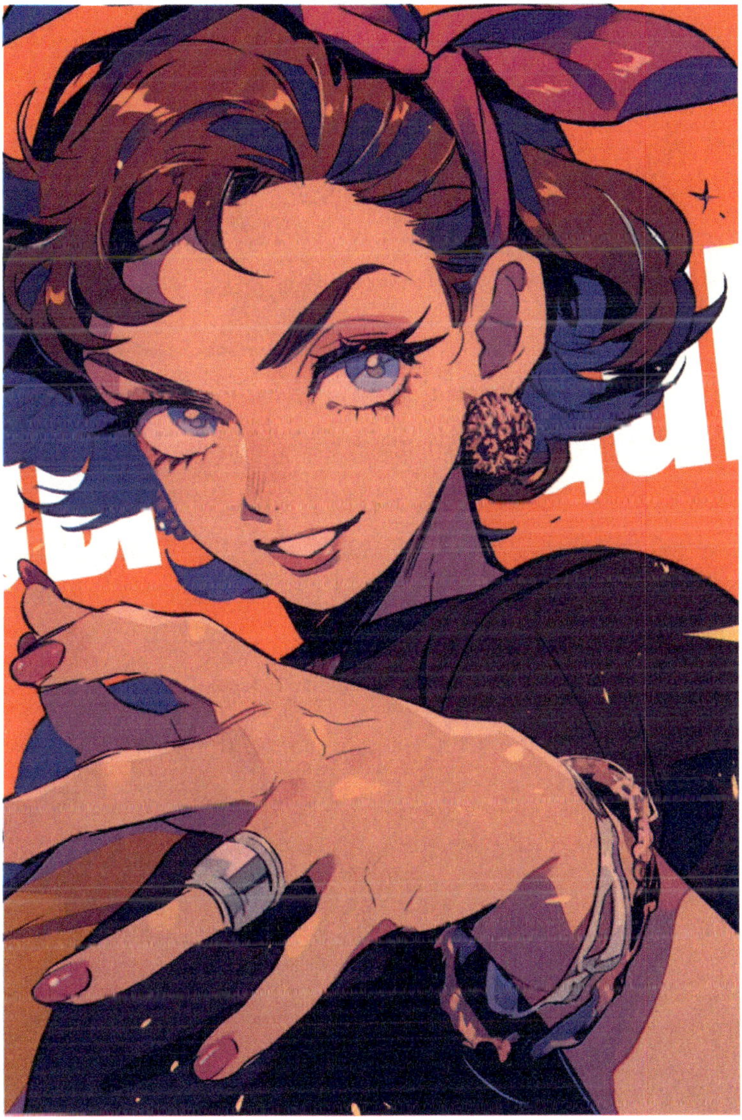

chapter 25

Tributes and remembrances from fans and celebrities

Throughout her career and beyond, Judy Garland was adored and admired by fans and celebrities alike. Her raw talent, undeniable charisma, and genuine vulnerability resonated deeply with people from all walks of life. As news of her passing in 1969 spread, the world mourned the loss of a true icon.

Fans, unable to contain their grief, flocked to various places to pay tribute to their beloved star. The most notable location was the Stonewall Inn in New York City, where the LGBTQ+ community, who had grown to identify with Garland's struggles and triumphs, gathered to mourn her passing. This gathering turned into the historic Stonewall Riots, often credited as a catalyst for the modern LGBTQ+ rights movement.

From Hollywood to Broadway to music halls around the world, fellow performers paid homage to Garland. Her peers recognized her as a unique talent and a trailblazer in the industry. Frank Sinatra, a close friend of Garland's, once said, "She was the greatest entertainer that ever lived, and nobody will ever top that."

Celebrities sent their condolences and shared heartfelt memories of their experiences with Garland. Her co-stars, such as Mickey Rooney and Margaret O'Brien, praised her professionalism and dedication to her craft. They remarked upon her ability to capture an audience with her vulnerable yet powerful performances, leaving an indelible impact on all who watched her.

Judy's daughter, Liza Minnelli, who followed in her mother's footsteps, spoke openly about their complicated relationship but also expressed her deep love and admiration for her mother's talent. Liza continues to honor her mother's legacy through her own career, often citing her mother's influence on her artistry.

Fan clubs dedicated to Garland's memory sprang up all over the world. These devoted individuals formed a united community, bonding over their shared love for Judy. They organized annual gatherings, film screenings, and concerts, keeping her memory alive while introducing her to new generations of fans.

Over the years, numerous tribute concerts have been held in honor of Garland. Prominent artists, including Barbra Streisand, Bette Midler, and Rufus Wainwright, have paid homage to her by performing her iconic songs and capturing her essence on stage. These tributes serve as a testament to Garland's enduring musical legacy and her ability to connect with audiences in a profound way.

In addition to live performances, Garland's influence extends to adaptations onscreen. Numerous documentaries and biopics have been made to shed light on the complex life and career of Judy Garland. These productions aim to reintroduce her to a new generation of fans and ensure that her legacy continues to thrive.

Even today, fans continue to gather at Garland's final resting place in Hartsdale, New York, to pay their respects. They leave flowers, letters, and memorabilia as a tribute to the woman who touched so many lives with her artistry. Her influence is not restricted to one era or one demographic; it transcends generations and continues to inspire performers from all corners of the entertainment world.

Judy Garland's voice resonates through the ages, her vulnerability captivating hearts and souls. She not only paved the way for countless performers who came after her, but she also served as a beacon of hope and resilience for individuals who faced their own struggles. Her performances were not mere acts; they were transformative experiences, each one leaving an indelible mark on the collective consciousness of humanity.

Garland's memorable roles, such as Dorothy in "The Wizard of Oz," have become ingrained in popular culture. The film, though released in 1939, remains a beloved classic to this day, and Garland's rendition of "Somewhere Over the Rainbow" stands as a timeless anthem of hope and dreams. Her portrayal of Esther Blodgett in "A Star is Born" showcased her versatility and emotional range, earning her critical acclaim and further cementing her status as a Hollywood legend.

Yet, behind the glitz and glamour, Judy Garland faced personal demons and struggles. The pressures of fame, early stardom, and a demanding industry took a toll on her mental and physical well-being. Her battle with addiction and her turbulent relationships added layers of complexity to her public image. However, it was this vulnerability and authenticity that endeared her to fans, who found solace and comfort in her performances while empathizing with her own hardships.

Garland's career spanned several mediums, from film to television and stage. Her Broadway triumphs, particularly her acclaimed one woman show at the Palace Theater, showcased her astonishing talent and ability to hold an audience captive with a single spotlight and her voice. The energy she exuded on stage was unparalleled, and audiences were left in awe, feeling a connection to her spirit and the emotions she poured into her performances.

In the wake of her passing, Garland's legacy has continued to grow. Her influence can be seen and heard in the work of contemporary artists who draw inspiration from her fearlessness and vulnerability. She remains a muse to many, reminding performers that true artistry lies in authenticity and a willingness to explore the depths of human emotion.

Judy Garland, a force of nature, continues to be celebrated and remembered as a shining star in the entertainment industry. Her talent, resilience, and impact on the world are impossible to ignore. The tributes, gatherings, and artistic adaptations that honor her legacy ensure that her spirit lives on, inspiring new generations to embrace their own vulnerabilities and pursue their dreams with unwavering determination.

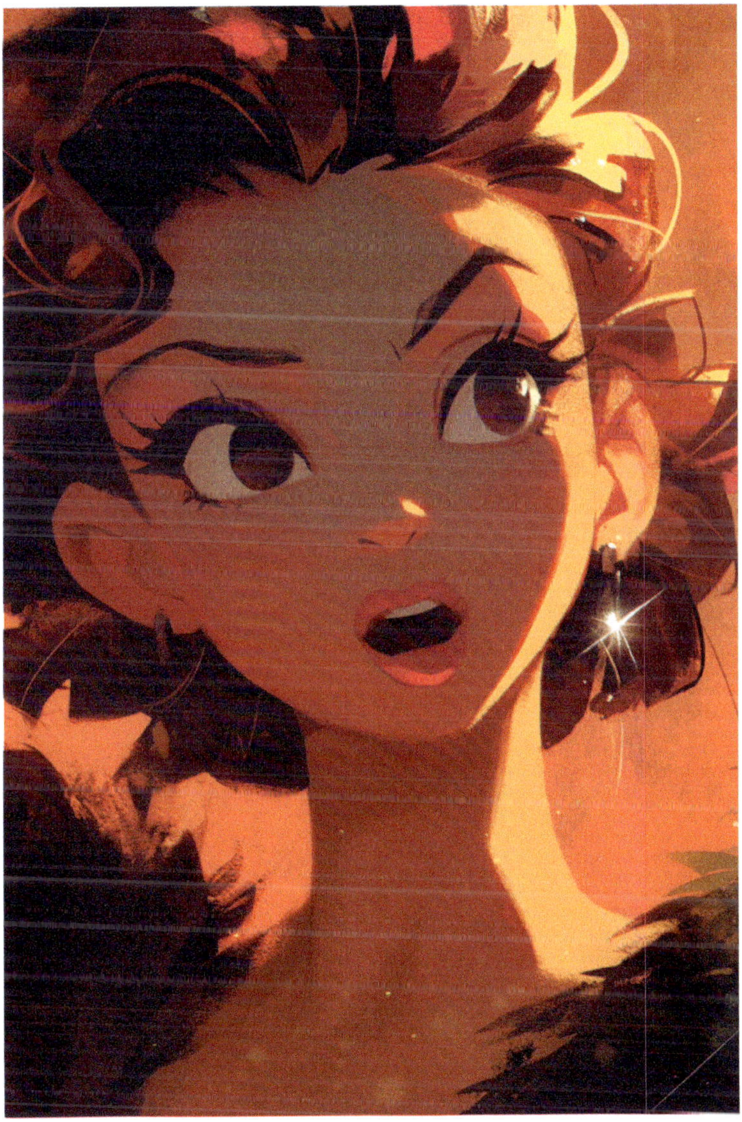

chapter 26

The preservation of Judy Garland's work and memorabilia

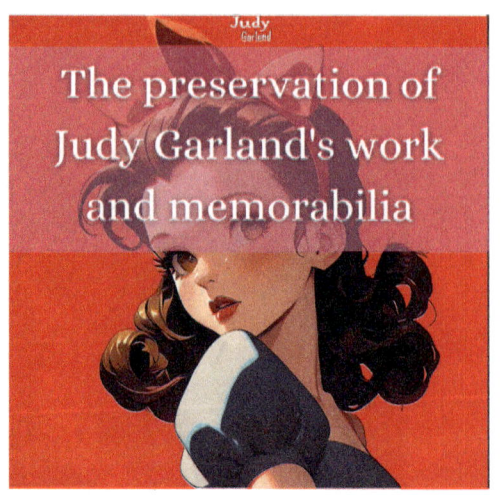

Throughout her illustrious career, Judy Garland left an indelible mark on the world of entertainment. As a beloved actress, singer, and performer, her contributions to film and music have become an integral part of American cultural history. However, the preservation of Garland's work and memorabilia has been a crucial endeavor to ensure that future generations can appreciate her talent and enduring legacy.

The importance of preserving Garland's work stems from its artistic and historical significance. Through her captivating performances on screen and stage, Garland showcased her exceptional talent and left an undeniable impact on audiences worldwide. From her iconic portrayal of Dorothy in "The Wizard of Oz" to her emotionally charged performances in "A Star is Born" and "Meet Me in St. Louis," her body of work represents a unique and timeless contribution to the film industry.

Preserving Garland's memorabilia, including costumes, personal items, and awards, is equally important in understanding her personal and professional journey. These artifacts provide valuable insights into the life and experiences of one of Hollywood's brightest stars. Costumes worn by Garland in iconic films like "The Wizard of Oz" are not simply pieces of clothing, but tangible symbols of her talent and the magic she brought to the screen. By preserving these items, we can connect with the past and appreciate the craftsmanship and artistry that went into creating such memorable moments.

Several institutions and organizations have dedicated themselves to the preservation of Judy Garland's work and memorabilia. The Smithsonian National Museum of American History has been at the forefront, playing a vital role in safeguarding Garland's legacy. Its Judy Garland Collection boasts an array of items associated with the actress, including costumes, film scripts, and personal effects. These artifacts are carefully cataloged, conserved, and displayed in temperature and humidity-controlled environments, ensuring their long-term preservation. Through interactive displays and audiovisual presentations, visitors can immerse themselves in the world of Judy Garland and gain a deeper understanding of her impact on the entertainment industry.

The Judy Garland Museum in Grand Rapids, Minnesota, serves as a comprehensive tribute to the star's humble beginnings and subsequent rise to stardom. Situated in Garland's childhood home, the museum allows visitors to step back in time and experience the surroundings that shaped her early life. The collection of personal belongings and memorabilia showcases the evolution of Garland's career, providing a glimpse into her journey from a child vaudeville performer to an internationally acclaimed actress. From her iconic blue gingham dress worn in "The Wizard of Oz" to candid family photographs, these items offer an intimate glimpse into Garland's personal and professional life.

However, the preservation of Garland's work and memorabilia is not limited to large institutions. Dedicated private collectors have also played a vital role in safeguarding her legacy. They scour auctions, estate sales, and private collections, seeking out rare and significant items associated with Garland. By providing a safe haven for these artifacts, collectors ensure their continued existence and accessibility to the public. Many collectors make their treasures available for exhibitions, allowing fans and enthusiasts to immerse themselves in the magic of Judy Garland's world.

Digital preservation has revolutionized the way Garland's work and memorabilia are shared with audiences worldwide. Through the digitization of films, photographs, and recordings, her performances can be preserved in their original form and made accessible to a larger audience. Online archives and streaming platforms serve as virtual preservation efforts, allowing fans from all corners of the globe to experience the magic of Garland's performances. These initiatives not only ensure the preservation of Garland's work but also serve as valuable educational resources for researchers, scholars, and fans alike, providing a comprehensive understanding of her artistry.

The preservation of Judy Garland's work and memorabilia not only honors her remarkable contributions to the entertainment world but also carries economic implications. The popularity and enduring fame of Garland's contributions have led to a robust market for her memorabilia. Authentic costumes, personal items, and signed collectibles have become highly sought-after by avid Garland enthusiasts, collectors, and investors alike. Through auctions, exhibitions, and licensing agreements, the preservation of Garland's artifacts contributes to the economy while further solidifying her place in cultural history.

In conclusion, the preservation of Judy Garland's work and memorabilia is an intricate process involving numerous institutions, collectors, and digital platforms. By safeguarding her films, memorabilia, and personal items, we ensure that her incredible talent and enduring legacy are preserved and celebrated for generations to come. Whether in the halls of museums, the hands of collectors, or the digital realm, the magic of Judy Garland's performances will continue to inspire, entertain, and captivate audiences worldwide. Through these preservation efforts, we pay homage to the remarkable artistry and impact of one of Hollywood's brightest stars.

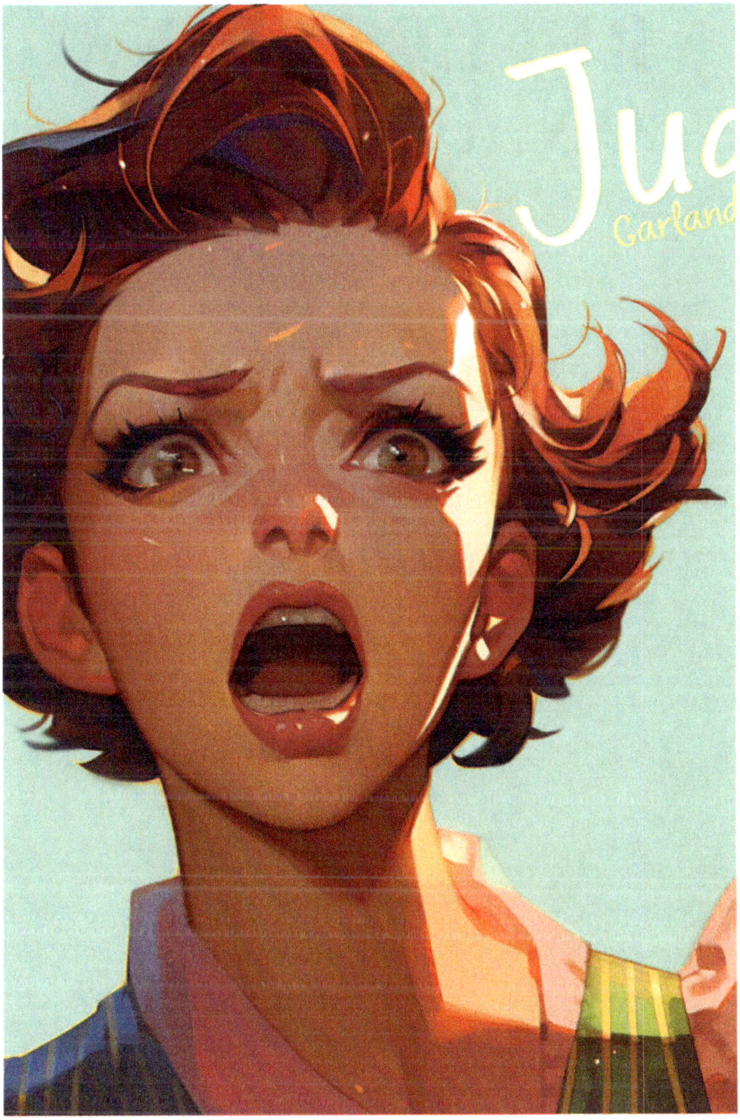
Ju
Garland

REFLECTIONS ON A LEGEND

chapter 27

Analysis of Garland's influence on the film industry and popular culture

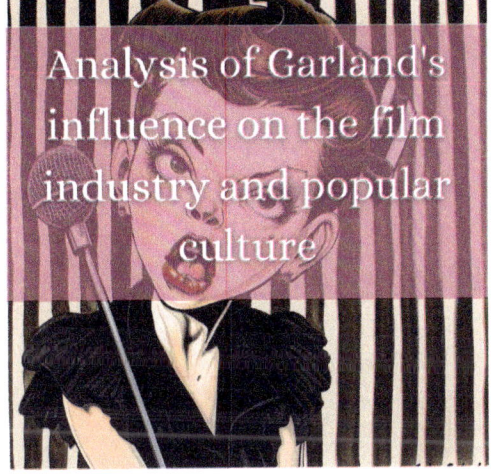

Judy Garland's impact on the film industry and popular culture cannot be overstated. Her talent, charisma, and unique voice revolutionized the entertainment world, leaving an indelible mark that continues to resonate to this day.

Garland's career spanned decades, and during that time, she showcased her versatility as an actress, a singer, and a performer. Her ability to convey raw emotion and vulnerability on screen was unparalleled, drawing audiences into her performances and allowing them to connect with her on a deeply personal level. This genuine connection is what made Garland a pillar of the film industry.

One of the key elements of Garland's influence lies in her ability to captivate both young and old audiences. Her breakout role as Dorothy Gale in "The Wizard of Oz" catapulted her into stardom and showcased her innate talent at a young age. The film's magical world and Garland's heartfelt rendition of "Over the Rainbow" seamlessly intertwined to create a timeless masterpiece. Garland's portrayal of Dorothy was so iconic and relatable that every generation since then has been enchanted by her performance.

Beyond "The Wizard of Oz," Garland continued to establish herself as a force to be reckoned with. Her roles in films such as "Meet Me in St. Louis," "A Star is Born," and "Judgment at Nuremberg" solidified her status as a versatile and talented actress. She effortlessly transitioned between musicals, dramas, and comedies, proving her range and leaving audiences and critics in awe. Garland's character in "Meet Me in St. Louis," Esther Smith, became a symbol of resilience and family values, resonating with audiences during a time of war and uncertainty.

In addition to her acting prowess, Garland's influence in the music industry cannot be understated. Her rich and expressive voice, filled with a blend of vulnerability and strength, resonated with millions of fans worldwide. Garland's seamless integration of songs into her film roles created groundbreaking moments that broke traditional barriers. Her performance of "The Man That Got Away" in "A Star is Born" remains a masterclass in emotional storytelling through song. Her signature songs, such as "Over the Rainbow," "Get Happy," and "Have Yourself a Merry Little Christmas," became anthems of hope, resilience, and introspection, winning her the admiration and love of countless fans.

Garland's impact went beyond her performances on screen and stage. She had a profound effect on popular culture, inspiring generations of artists in various disciplines. Many performers, from Barbra Streisand and Liza Minnelli to Freddie Mercury and Lady Gaga, have cited Garland as a major influence on their careers. Streisand, for example, was not only inspired by Garland's singing style but also looked up to her as a versatile actress. Minnelli, Garland's daughter, followed in her mother's footsteps, establishing her own successful career in the entertainment industry. Mercury admired Garland's ability to connect emotionally with her audience and incorporated elements of her performance style into his own captivating stage presence. Lady Gaga, a self-proclaimed Garland fan, paid homage to the icon with her 2019 role in "A Star is Born," proving that Garland's influence transcends generations.

Moreover, Garland's legacy extends beyond her talent and on-screen presence. Her struggles with personal demons, including addiction and mental health issues, have become part of her story, allowing others to find solace and inspiration in her journey. Garland's courage in openly addressing and confronting her challenges served as a beacon of hope for those facing similar obstacles. Her resilience and determination to overcome adversity resonated with fans and encouraged a wider conversation about the importance of mental health awareness and support in the entertainment industry.

In conclusion, Judy Garland's influence on the film industry and popular culture is immeasurable. Her talent, passion, and authenticity continue to inspire and captivate audiences today. Whether it be through her iconic performances, her unforgettable voice, or her personal journey, Garland's impact remains a testament to her enduring legacy as a true Hollywood legend. Through her artistry, Garland touched the lives of countless individuals, leaving an indelible mark on the history of film and popular culture.

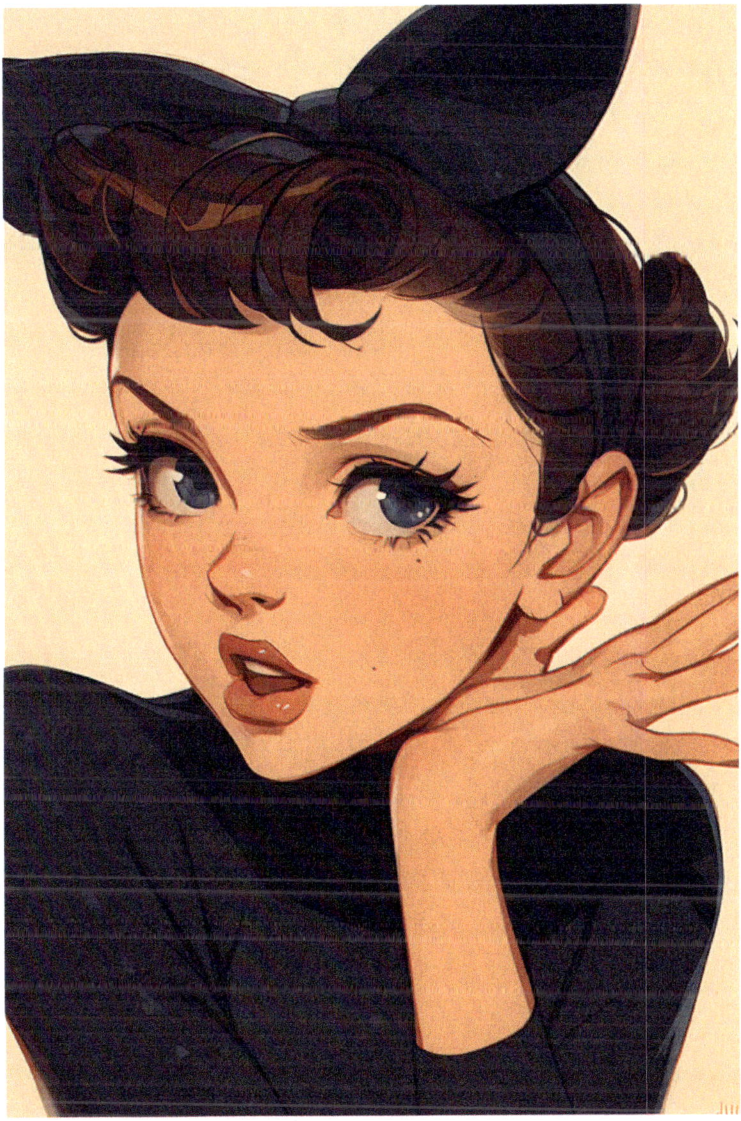

chapter 28

The significance of Garland's journey in the broader context of Hollywood's evolution

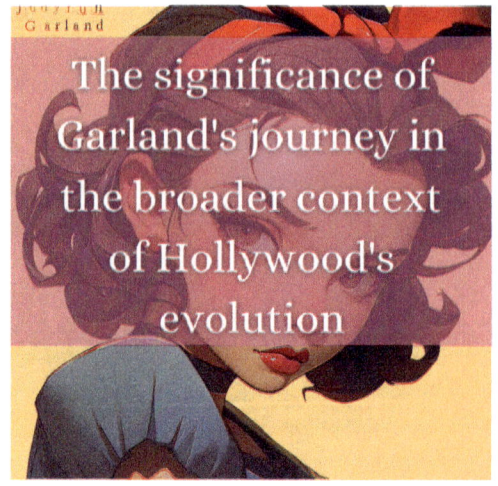

Judy Garland's journey through the entertainment industry holds immense significance in the broader context of Hollywood's evolution. Her rise to stardom and enduring popularity symbolize the changing landscape of the film industry and the shifting perceptions of female talent during her era.

During the 1930s and 1940s, Hollywood was primarily dominated by male actors, and female stars were often constrained by constricting gender stereotypes. However, Garland stood out as an exceptional talent who defied these limitations. She possessed an extraordinary ability to portray characters with depth, vulnerability, and strength, breaking free from the confines of the traditional female roles of the time.

One of Garland's most iconic roles, Dorothy in **The Wizard of Oz**, showcased her ability to captivate audiences with her enchanting innocence and powerful emotional range. Her portrayal of Dorothy became a symbol of hope and resilience, resonating with viewers who themselves longed for adventure and a sense of belonging. Garland's interpretation of the character went beyond mere performance; it became a cultural touchstone, elevating the film to legendary status and asserting her influence as a leading lady capable of commanding the screen and shaping the narrative.

Garland's exceptional talent was not limited to one role; it spanned a wide range of films and genres. In **Meet Me in St. Louis**, she delivered a nuanced performance as Esther Smith, capturing the complexities of a young woman experiencing love, heartbreak, and familial bonds. Her vivaciousness and genuine emotions created a connection with audiences that transcended the screen, making her relatable and beloved.

Moreover, Garland's abilities extended beyond acting alone. She possessed an extraordinary voice, a captivating instrument that had the power to move audiences to tears or bring them to their feet in thunderous applause. Her signature songs, such as "Over the Rainbow," became anthems of hope and dreams, encapsulating the collective desires of a generation yearning for brighter possibilities. Garland's voice was a testament to her artistry, combining technical prowess with an emotional depth that resonated with listeners. Her ability to imbue each lyric with a raw, passionate energy made her performances unforgettable.

Beyond her on-screen accomplishments, Garland's personal struggles and triumphs also forged her legacy as a groundbreaking figure. Throughout her career, she faced the volatile nature of the entertainment industry, battling with addiction, mental health issues, and body image pressures. In an era where the private lives of celebrities were heavily curated, Garland's candor and vulnerability were revolutionary. By sharing her own challenges, she humanized the Hollywood star and shed light on the hidden realities behind the glamour and fame. Her openness not only paved the way for greater understanding and compassion toward mental health, but also exposed the immense pressures faced by entertainers, leading to a collective examination of the toll of stardom on mental well-being.

Garland's journey also represented a pivotal shift in the Hollywood system. She emerged during a time when the legendary studio systems held significant control over actors and their careers. Yet, Garland's rise to fame and enduring success symbolized the growing importance of an actor's individuality and connection with their audience. While initially signed to Metro-Goldwyn-Mayer (MGM) under an exclusive contract, Garland's exceptional talent allowed her to break free from the studio's grip and assert her own creative autonomy. Her influence and popularity contributed to the dismantling of the studio system, as actors began to challenge the industry's traditional power structure and demand greater artistic freedom.

In retrospect, Judy Garland's journey exemplifies a transformative era in Hollywood where traditional gender roles, studio control, and societal expectations were being questioned and redefined. She left an indelible mark on the industry, not only through her artistry but also through her unyielding resilience and authenticity. As a trailblazer and cultural icon, Garland's influence continues to resonate in today's industry, reminding us of the ongoing fight for equal opportunities, representation, and the power of individuality. Her journey signifies a turning point in Hollywood's evolving narrative, where actresses like her defied conventions, shattered glass ceilings, and opened doors for future generations to follow their own paths toward success.

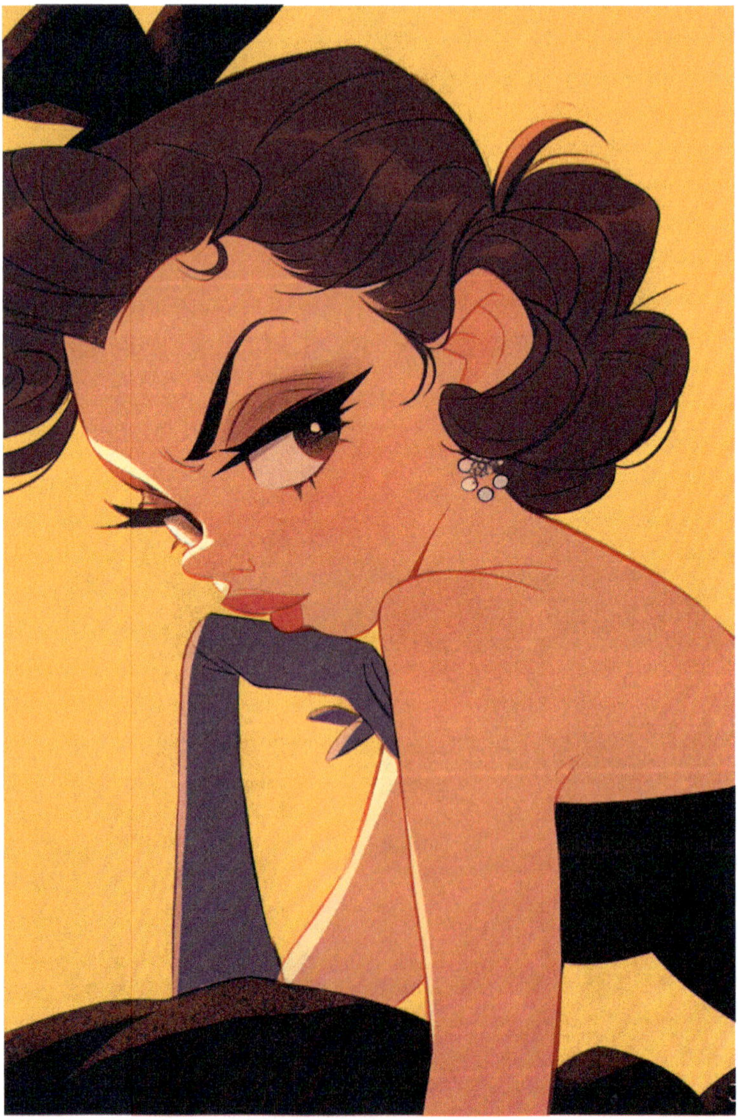

chapter 29

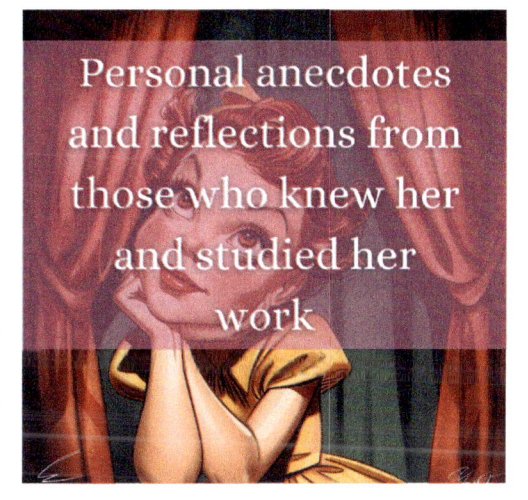

Personal anecdotes and reflections from those who knew her and studied her work

Throughout her life, Judy Garland captivated audiences with her extraordinary talent and magnetic presence. Those who had the privilege to know her and work with her have shared countless personal anecdotes and reflections on their experiences with the legendary performer. Additionally, many researchers, scholars, and fans have studied and analyzed Garland's work, providing unique and profound insights into her artistry and the profound impact she had on the world of entertainment.

1. Colleagues and Co-Stars:

- One of Judy Garland's closest friends and co-stars, Mickey Rooney, once said, "Judy had an uncanny ability to light up a room with her energy. Whether we were rehearsing or performing, she gave her all and had an infectious enthusiasm that sparked everyone around her. Working with her was always a joyous experience." Rooney's sentiment is a testament to Garland's vibrant spirit and the energy she exuded, which undoubtedly contributed to her captivating performances.

- Gene Kelly, who had the privilege of working alongside Garland in films like **For Me and My Gal** and **The Pirate**, commented on her exceptional depth as an artist. He said, "Judy possessed an innate vulnerability and depth that brought something special to every performance. She was a perfectionist and had a deep understanding of the characters she portrayed. She worked tirelessly to bring their emotional truth to the screen. She gave her heart and soul to the work, and it was truly inspiring to witness." Kelly's words emphasize the immense dedication and emotional investment Garland brought to her craft, elevating her performances to unforgettable heights.

- Margaret O'Brien, who portrayed Garland's on-screen sister in **Meet Me in St. Louis**, affectionately shared, "Judy was like a second mother to me during the filming of **Meet Me in St. Louis**. She was incredibly caring, nurturing, and generous with her time and advice. She made sure we felt comfortable and supported on set, creating a family-like atmosphere that translated onto the screen." Garland's ability to create a supportive and inclusive environment speaks to her empathetic nature, and this nurturing environment undoubtedly contributed to the film's timeless charm and emotional resonance.

2. Directors and Collaborators:

- Vincente Minnelli, an acclaimed director who had the privilege of being Garland's second husband and directing her in films like **Meet Me in St. Louis** and **The Clock**, had profound admiration for her artistic capabilities. He said, "Working with Judy was an absolute privilege. Not only was she a phenomenal actress and singer, but she had an intuitive understanding of character and storytelling. She had an immense emotional range and knew how to channel it into her performances. She brought depth and subtlety to her roles, captivating audiences with her authenticity. Her ability to emotionally connect with the audience was unrivaled." Minnelli's appreciation for Garland's multifaceted skills as an artist and her ability to emotionally resonate with audiences showcases her versatility and the depth she brought to her performances.

- George Cukor, director of the classic film **A Star is Born**, remarked on Garland's fearlessness as a performer. He commented, "Judy's performance in **A Star is Born** was one of the most honest and raw portrayals I've ever witnessed. She fearlessly exposed her vulnerabilities, allowing the audience to connect with her on a deeply personal level. She was willing to take risks and push herself as an artist, and her dedication and commitment were awe-inspiring." Garland's willingness to delve into the complexities of human emotion and expose her own vulnerabilities undoubtedly contributed to the profound impact she had on audiences worldwide.

- Irving Berlin, the iconic songwriter who wrote "Over the Rainbow" for **The Wizard of Oz**, once expressed his admiration for Garland's rendition of the song. He said, "Judy's rendition of my song was pure magic. She captured the essence of longing and hope with her voice, making it one of the most moving moments in cinematic history. Her ability to infuse a song with emotion was unparalleled, and she had a unique way of making the audience feel seen and understood." Berlin's insight shines a light on Garland's remarkable vocal abilities and her ability to convey deep emotions through her music, imprinting her performances on the hearts of generations.

3. Researchers and Scholars:
- Dr. Susan Mayer, a Garland biographer and esteemed scholar, dedicated extensive research to understanding the significance of Garland's artistic contributions. She noted, "Judy Garland's ability to convey emotion through her voice was unparalleled. She had a voice that could express every shade of emotion, from heartbreak to joy, and it resonated deeply with audiences. Her vulnerability and authenticity touched the hearts of millions, creating a profound impact that extends far beyond the screen. She was a true master of her craft." Dr. Mayer's profound appreciation for Garland's emotional resonance underscores the lasting impact of her performances and validates the admiration shared by countless fans.

- Dr. David Harris, a film studies professor, delved into Judy Garland's legacy as an actress and artist. He commented, "Garland's performances were a masterclass in authenticity and vulnerability. She understood the power of subtlety and nuance, and her ability to convey complex emotions through her acting and singing revolutionized the way we perceive on-screen performances. She took risks and exposed her own vulncrabilities, pushing the boundaries of what was expected from a performer in her time." Dr. Harris's analysis sheds light on Garland's contributions to the evolution of acting techniques, as well as her courage in challenging societal norms and expectations in pursuit of deeply authentic portrayals.

- Furthermore, the online fan community has an abundance of personal stories reflecting the enduring impact of Judy Garland's work. Fans have shared how her performances provided comfort, inspiration, and a sense of belonging during difficult times. They admire how she overcame personal struggles and used her art to connect with people on a deep level. Judy Garland's legacy continues to inspire future generations of performers as her vulnerable yet powerful performances continue to resonate with audiences.

These personal anecdotes and reflections from those who knew Judy Garland, colleagues, directors, scholars, and fans alike, reveal the depths of her influence as an artist and person. Each account adds another layer to understanding Garland's immense talent, dedication, and the profound impact she had on those around her. Judy Garland's ability to touch hearts, convey authenticity and vulnerability, and create a lasting emotional impact is what solidifies her status as one of the most revered and beloved figures in the entertainment industry.

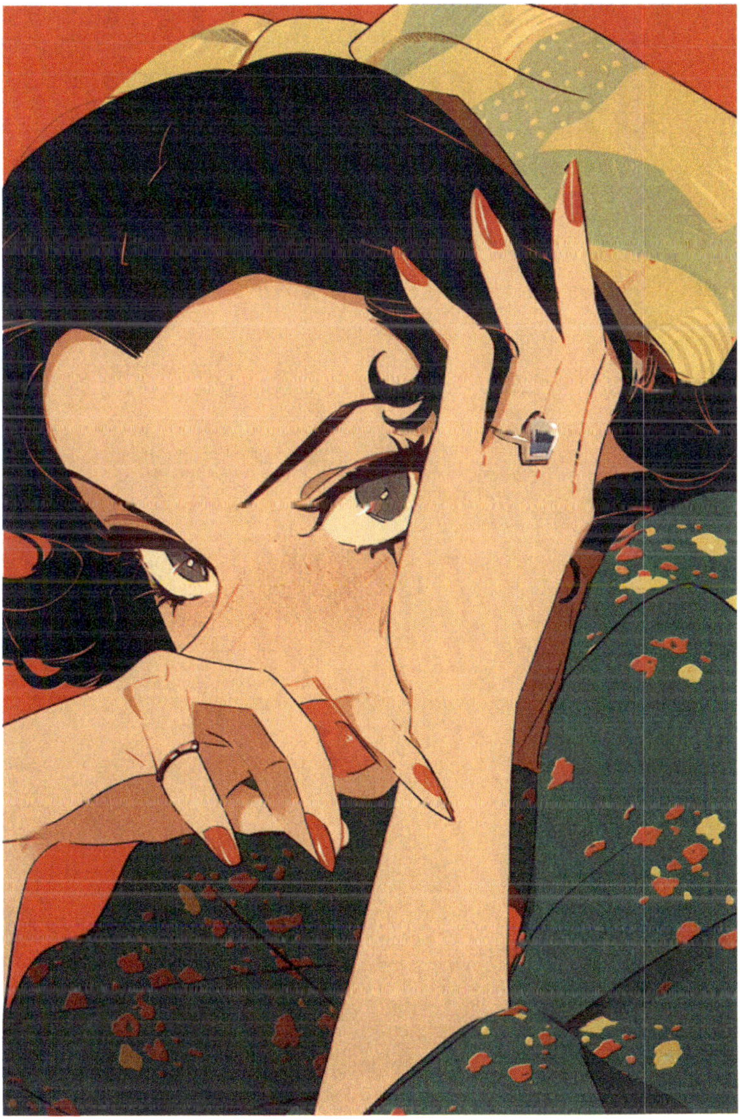

CONCLUSION: BEYOND THE RAINBOW

chapter 30

Summarizing Garland's journey from a young girl in Minnesota to a Hollywood legend

Judy Garland's journey from a young girl in Minnesota to a Hollywood legend is a captivating story of talent, perseverance, and struggle. Born Frances Ethel Gumm on June 10, 1922, in Grand Rapids, Minnesota, Garland showed an early passion for singing and performing. Her incredible voice and stage presence caught the attention of industry professionals, leading her family to move to California in pursuit of her dreams.

In the early years of her career, Garland faced numerous challenges. She worked tirelessly, auditioning and performing in various venues, including vaudeville acts and small film roles. It was during this time that she honed her skills and developed her signature style—the combination of vulnerability, strength, and emotion that would captivate audiences for decades to come.

Garland's breakthrough came when she signed with MGM at the age of 13. The studio recognized her immense talent and potential, but also exerted strict control over her image and career. They soon changed her name to Judy Garland, a name that symbolized her transformation into a star.

Under the guidance of MGM, Garland flourished as a performer. Her natural talent, combined with extensive training in acting, singing, and dancing, made her a force to be reckoned with. Despite her young age, Garland displayed a maturity and depth in her performances that belied her years. She had the ability to convey a wide range of emotions, from joy to heartache, with an authenticity that resonated deeply with audiences.

It was during this period that Garland became a true triple threat in the entertainment industry. She not only starred in films but also performed on stage and recorded music, showcasing her versatility as an artist. Her live shows were renowned for their electrifying energy and emotional intensity. Whether she was belting out a show-stopping number or tenderly interpreting a ballad, Garland's presence onstage was magnetic, capturing the hearts of all who witnessed her talent.

However, it was her iconic role as Dorothy Gale in "The Wizard of Oz" that solidified Garland's place in Hollywood history. Released in 1939, the film became an instant classic, with Garland's portrayal of the young girl from Kansas capturing the hearts of audiences around the world. Her rendition of "Over the Rainbow" became her signature song, symbolizing both Garland's personal struggles and the hopes and dreams of a generation.

Behind the scenes, Garland faced personal challenges that often threatened to overshadow her professional success. The pressures of fame, combined with a demanding work schedule, took a toll on her mental and physical well-being. She struggled with self-doubt, seeking approval and validation from others. Studio executives at MGM constantly monitored her weight and appearance, leading to an unhealthy relationship with food and a reliance on prescription medication.

Despite these battles, Garland continued to shine in her work. Her raw vulnerability and emotional depth made her performances unforgettable. In films like "The Harvey Girls" and "Easter Parade," she showcased her comedic timing and natural charm, proving that she could excel in a variety of roles. Garland's talent was undeniable, and her ability to tap into the complexities of the human experience resonated with audiences on a deeply personal level.

As time went on, Garland transitioned to television and live performances, where she could truly connect with her fans in an intimate setting. These shows became legendary, as Garland poured her heart and soul into each performance, creating a bond with her audience that transcended the boundaries of the stage. Despite the challenges she faced in her personal life, Garland's determination to bring joy to others through her art never wavered.

At the same time, Garland's personal life was marked by struggles and heartbreak. She experienced tumultuous relationships, including marriages to musician David Rose, film director Vincente Minnelli, and businessman Sidney Luft. These relationships were often plagued by turmoil and ended in divorce. Garland's personal struggles with mental health and substance abuse further complicated her life, at times overshadowing her professional success.

However, despite the hardships she faced, Garland's talent continued to shine. In 1954, she delivered a career-defining performance in the musical drama "A Star is Born." Her portrayal of Esther Blodgett/Vicki Lester earned her critical acclaim and renewed public adoration. The film showcased Garland's extraordinary range as an actress and singer, cementing her status as an icon of the silver screen.

Throughout her career, Garland cultivated a devoted fan base that spanned generations. Her impact on future artists is immeasurable, with performers like Barbra Streisand and Lady Gaga citing Garland as a major influence on their work. Her tremendous legacy lives on through her timeless recordings, cherished film performances, and profound influence on the entertainment industry as a whole.

Tragically, Garland's life was cut short at the age of 47, when she passed away on June 22, 1969. While her untimely death marked an end to her own personal journey, her impact and influence have endured. Today, Judy Garland is remembered not only as a remarkable talent but also as a symbol of resilience, perseverance, and the enduring power of art to touch the lives of millions.

In summarizing Garland's journey from a young girl in Minnesota to a Hollywood legend, it is evident that her talent, resilience, and enduring spirit propelled her to greatness. Through her music, film performances, and live shows, she connected with audiences on a profound level, leaving an indelible mark on the world of entertainment. Judy Garland's legacy continues to inspire and captivate, reminding us of the transformative power of dreams, determination, and the extraordinary impact one individual can have.

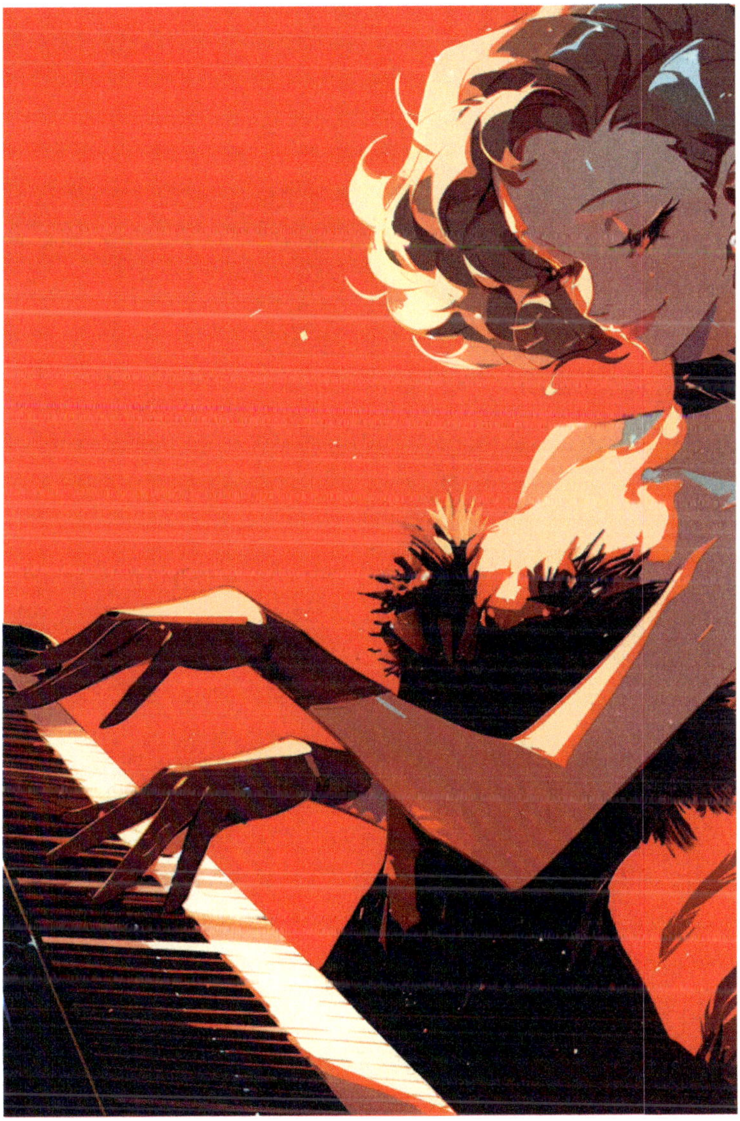

chapter 31

Reflecting on the enduring qualities that make Garland a timeless icon

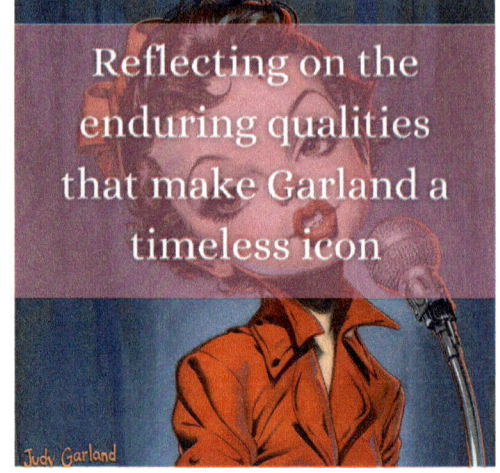

Judy Garland's legacy as an icon transcends time and continues to captivate audiences around the world. Her unique combination of talent, vulnerability, authenticity, and advocacy has secured her a permanent place in the annals of Hollywood history. In this extended chapter, we will delve deeper into the enduring qualities that make Garland such a beloved and timeless figure.

One of Garland's most notable qualities is her unparalleled talent. Born Frances Ethel Gumm in 1922, she began performing at a very young age alongside her talented sisters as part of the vaudeville act, The Gumm Sisters. It was evident even then that she possessed a remarkable voice that could convey a wide range of emotions and captivate audiences with its power and beauty. As she transitioned from a child star to a young adult, Garland's talent blossomed, and she quickly became a force to be reckoned with in the entertainment industry. Her exceptional vocal ability, particularly her ability to infuse emotion into each note, made her stand out amongst her peers. Whether she was belting out show-stopping numbers or delicately conveying vulnerability through a soft ballad, Garland's voice had an undeniable impact on all who heard it.

However, it was through Garland's vulnerability that she truly touched the hearts of audiences. Throughout her career, she bared her soul on screen, allowing audiences to glimpse her raw emotions. From her breakthrough role as Dorothy Gale in "The Wizard of Oz" to her complex and heartbreaking portrayal of Esther Blodgett/Vicki Lester in "A Star Is Born," Garland had a way of connecting with viewers on a deeply emotional level. It was as if she wore her heart on her sleeve, making audiences feel as if they were experiencing her joys and struggles alongside her. Garland's vulnerability wasn't just apparent on screen; it was an integral part of her personal life as well. She faced numerous challenges, including a demanding work schedule, marital difficulties, and battles with mental health. Yet, she continued to put herself out there, pouring her heart and soul into everything she did. This transparency endeared her to fans who appreciated her honesty and the courage it took for her to share her struggles with the world.

In addition to her talent and vulnerability, Garland's authenticity is a crucial element of her iconic status. In an era when the Hollywood studio system tightly controlled and constructed many stars' public images, Garland refused to conform and remained true to herself. Her unapologetic authenticity set her apart from her contemporaries. Garland embraced both her strengths and flaws, allowing audiences to see the real person beneath the glamor and stardust. Her vulnerability and self-awareness, coupled with her immense talent, made her relatable. Whether she was performing live or interacting with fans off-stage, Garland's authenticity shone through. She didn't hide her imperfections, but rather celebrated them as part of what made her unique and human. This genuine approach allowed people to connect with her on a deeper level, breaking down barriers and fostering a deep and lasting connection.

Moreover, Garland's impact extends beyond the realm of entertainment. She became an unwitting advocate for mental health and LGBTQ+ rights, using her own personal struggles to shed light on important social issues. Garland's battles with depression, addiction, and a tumultuous personal life were often publicized, but she persisted and showed tremendous resilience. Her willingness to face these challenges head-on, while maintaining her vibrant spirit and magnetic presence, inspired countless individuals who were grappling with their own hardships. Garland's struggles helped destigmatize conversations around mental health and encouraged others to seek help and support without shame or fear. In addition, Garland became an unexpected ally to the LGBTQ+ community, as her status as a gay icon soared after her tragic passing. Her heartfelt performances and unwavering support for her gay fans made her an icon within the community and a symbol of acceptance and love.

As we reflect on Judy Garland's enduring qualities, it becomes clear that she was more than just a talented entertainer. She was a symbol of resilience, authenticity, vulnerability, and social change. Her influence can be seen in the performances of countless actors and musicians who have been inspired by her, and her impact on American culture is immeasurable. Garland's legacy serves as a testament to the power of honesty, vulnerability, and staying true to oneself. She will forever hold a cherished place in the hearts of her countless fans, and her light will continue to shine bright beyond the rainbow.

In conclusion, Judy Garland's enduring qualities as a timeless icon are rooted in her extraordinary talent, vulnerability, authenticity, and advocacy. From her early years as part of The Gumm Sisters to her iconic status as the girl next door in "The Wizard of Oz" and her transformative role in "A Star Is Born," Garland's talent was undeniable. She had a voice that could soar to unimaginable heights, and her ability to convey emotion through her performances was unparalleled. Garland's vulnerability and willingness to share her struggles endeared her to audiences, creating a deep connection that spanned generations. Her authenticity, refusing to conform to societal expectations, made her relatable and relished by fans worldwide. Furthermore, Garland's impact extended beyond the stage and screen. She unintentionally became an advocate for mental health and a beloved figure in the LGBTQ+ community. Her openness about her own battles with mental health broke barriers and inspired others to seek help. The love and acceptance she showed towards her gay fans made her an enduring symbol of hope and inclusivity. Judy Garland's legacy will continue to inspire and uplift individuals around the world, reminding us of the transformative power of vulnerability, authenticity, and staying true to oneself.

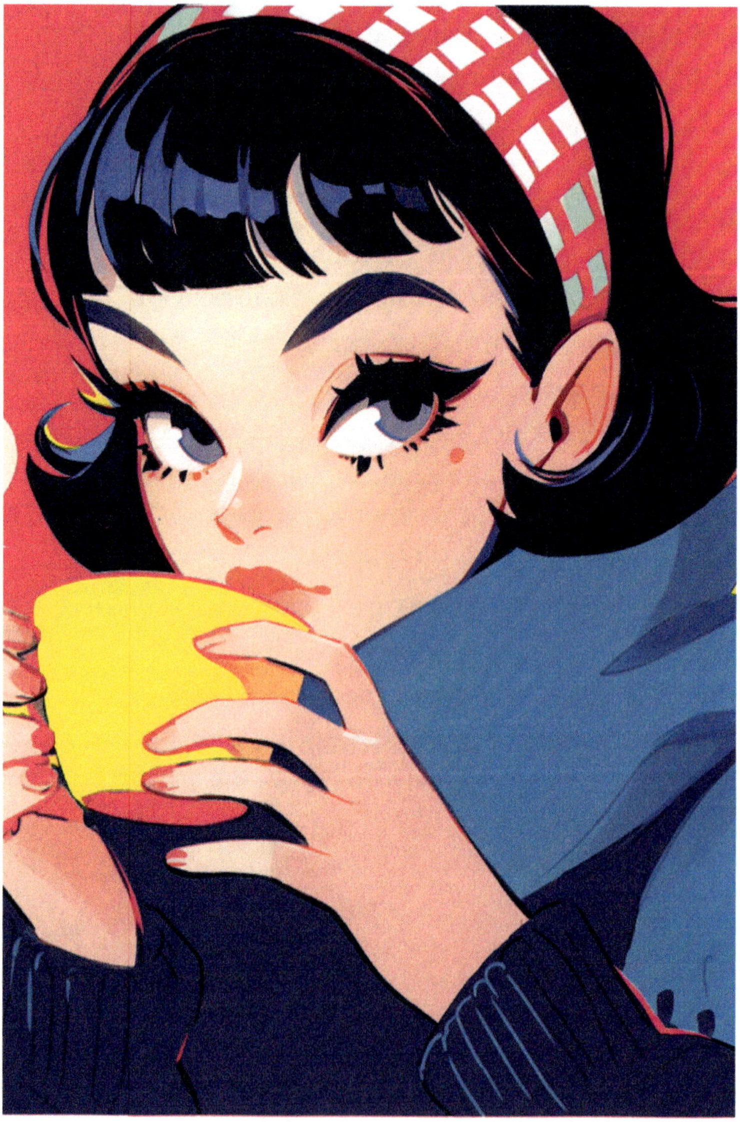

chapter 32

The role of **The Wizard of Oz** and Garland's subsequent work in shaping American culture

The impact of **The Wizard of Oz** on American culture cannot be overstated. Released in 1939, the film quickly achieved icon status and remains a beloved classic to this day, capturing the imaginations of both children and adults alike. At the center of this cultural phenomenon was Judy Garland and her unforgettable portrayal of Dorothy Gale, a role that would forever be associated with her and solidify her place in entertainment history.

First and foremost, **The Wizard of Oz** introduced Garland's incredible talent to the world. Born Frances Ethel Gumm in 1922, Garland had been performing since a young age, having been pushed by her ambitious stage mother, Ethel Gumm. However, Garland's journey towards stardom was not without its challenges. Her personal life was often plagued by struggles, including a difficult relationship with her mother, a tumultuous love life, and battles with addiction and mental health issues. Yet, through it all, Garland's unwavering dedication to her craft propelled her to greatness.

It was her breakthrough performance as Dorothy that showcased her exceptional abilities. Through her portrayal, Garland showcased her unmatched vocal prowess, bringing to life iconic songs like "Over the Rainbow" and "Somewhere Over the Rainbow." These timeless melodies, infused with her pure and emotive voice, reverberated with audiences, resonating deeply with their hopes, dreams, and longing for a place where troubles melt like lemon drops.

Garland's vulnerability and authenticity in portraying Dorothy had a profound effect on the representation of female characters in film. At a time when women were often relegated to the sidelines or portrayed as damsels in distress, Dorothy Gale became a role model for countless young girls. She embodied strength, resilience, and determination, single-handedly leading her companions through challenging trials and ultimately achieving her goal of returning home. Dorothy showed audiences that girls could be the heroes of their own stories and paved the way for future female protagonists who could break free from restrictive stereotypes.

Beyond her iconic role in **The Wizard of Oz**, Garland's subsequent work continued to shape American culture. Her performances in films like **Meet Me in St. Louis**, **Easter Parade**, and **A Star is Born** solidified her status as a versatile and influential actress. In these films, Garland displayed her acting range and ability to convey a vast array of emotions, captivating audiences with her authenticity and vulnerability. As an actress, she embodied the struggles and triumphs of ordinary people, making her characters relatable and leaving a lasting impact on viewers.

Garland's on-screen presence was magnetic, capturing the hearts of viewers and leaving an indelible mark on American cinema. Her performances were emotionally charged, often intertwining joy, sadness, and longing. In films like **A Star is Born**, she portrayed the complex journey of an aspiring actress, showcasing her remarkable ability to convey vulnerability, ambition, and heartbreak. Garland's talent to evoke genuine emotions in her audience made her a true star, beloved for her ability to connect with people on a deeply personal level.

Furthermore, Garland's impact reached beyond the world of film. Her contributions to the music industry, particularly with her live performances and studio recordings, left an indelible mark on American music. In addition to her success as an actress, she was also an accomplished singer and performer. Garland's voice possessed a unique quality that seamlessly transitioned between melancholy and joyousness, often imbuing her performances with an intense emotional resonance. Her ability to connect with audiences on a deeply personal and relatable level made her a true star of the silver screen and the recording studio.

Garland's personal struggles and triumphs also contributed to her cultural significance. Her openness about her battles with addiction, self-doubt, and mental health issues challenged societal stigmas and paved the way for greater understanding and empathy. Through her vulnerability and willingness to share her own journey, Garland became a champion for mental health advocacy, shedding light on the importance of seeking help and breaking down barriers in discussions surrounding mental well-being. In an era when such topics were often shrouded in secrecy, Garland's willingness to confront her own demons inspired and offered solace to countless individuals facing similar battles.

Even after her untimely passing at the age of 47, Garland's influence continues to be felt. Her timeless performances are still celebrated and studied, and her songs are constantly covered and reimagined by contemporary artists, ensuring her legacy endures. The impact of **The Wizard of Oz** and Garland's subsequent work can be witnessed in the countless tributes, adaptations, and homages paid to her throughout popular culture. Her authenticity, vulnerability, and unwavering commitment to her craft left an indelible mark on the entertainment industry and influenced generations to come.

In conclusion, **The Wizard of Oz** and Garland's subsequent work played a vital role in shaping American culture. Through her portrayal of Dorothy Gale and her subsequent achievements in film and music, Judy Garland not only became a household name but also a cultural icon. She will forever be remembered as a trailblazer, an emblem of hope, resilience, and the transformative power of art, whose impact continues to be felt long after her time. The legacy of Judy Garland serves as a testament to the enduring power of storytelling, the ability of one individual to touch the lives of millions, and the importance of confronting personal struggles with bravery and openness.

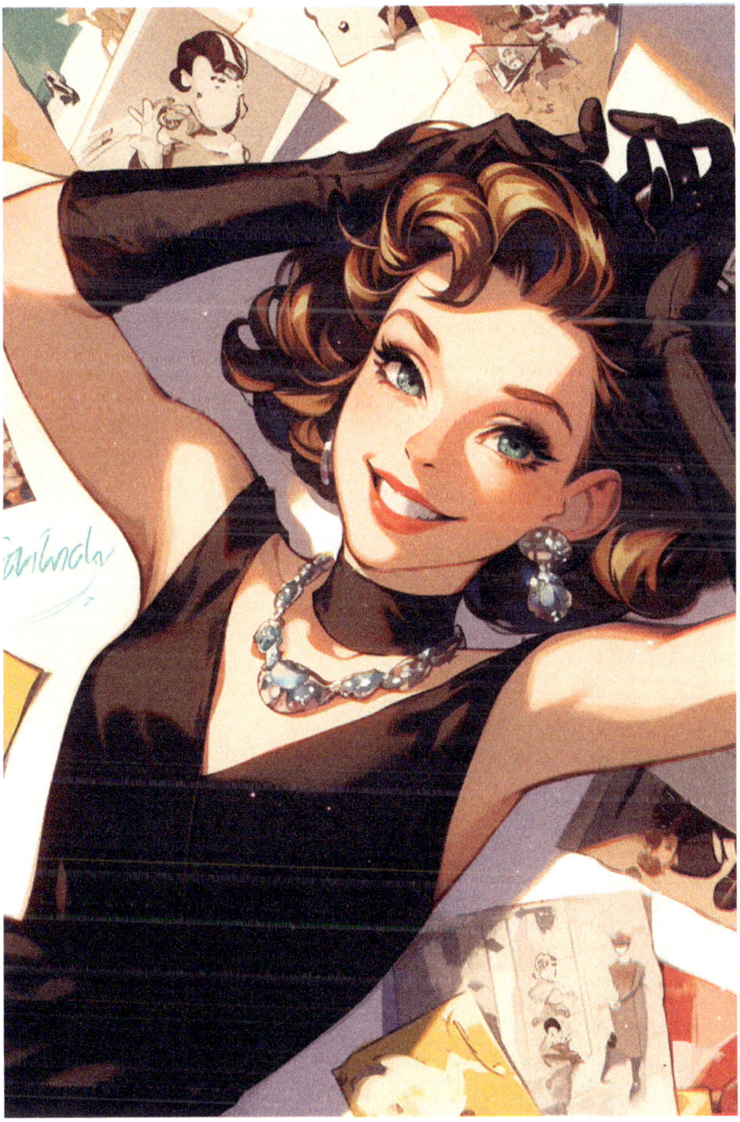